What people are

The Instagram Archipelago

'By way of a personal response to Idan Hayosh's deeply weird images, Elliot C. Mason has conjured a bracingly witty, original and lyrical meditation on architecture, fishing, bikinis and the possibility of escape from the "eclipsing wetness" of our homogenizing neoliberal culture.'
Josh Cohen, author of *Not Working: Why We Have to Stop*

'Elliot C. Mason is a force of nature. Dissolving the boundaries of genre, he provides a roadmap to the writing of the future. *The Instagram Archipelago* is witty, trenchant, and very very relevant.'
Frances Wilson, author of *The Ballad of Dorothy Wordsworth* and *The Courtesan's Revenge*

'Timely, insightful, moving, funny, and rigorous in its self-scrutiny. [Mason has written] a persuasive, and admirable, study of the white male gaze and the world it's helped bring about.'
Matt Greene, author of *Jew(ish)* and *Ostrich*

Also by the Author:

Building Black: Towards Antiracist Architecture (Punctum Books, 2021)

Materials for Building a City (Marble Books, 2021) ISBN: 978-1-9163369-6-4

City Embers (Death of Workers Whilst Building Skyscrapers, 2020/2021)

The Instagram Archipelago

Race, Gender, and the Lives of Dead Fish

The Instagram Archipelago

Race, Gender, and the Lives of Dead Fish

Elliot C. Mason

Winchester, UK
Washington, USA

JOHN HUNT PUBLISHING

First published by Zero Books, 2022
Zero Books is an imprint of John Hunt Publishing Ltd., No. 3 East St., Alresford,
Hampshire SO24 9EE, UK
office@jhpbooks.com
www.johnhuntpublishing.com
www.zero-books.net

For distributor details and how to order please visit the 'Ordering' section on our website.

ISBN: 978 1 78279 827 9
978 1 78279 828 6 (ebook)
Library of Congress Control Number: 2021942474

A CIP catalogue record for this book is available from the British Library.

Design: Stuart Davies

UK: Printed and bound by CPI Group (UK) Ltd, Croydon, CR0 4YY
Printed in North America by CPI GPS partners

We operate a distinctive and ethical publishing philosophy in
all areas of our business, from our global network of authors to
production and worldwide distribution.

Contents

For the fish, all the fish everywhere.

Acknowledgements

This book could not have existed without the obsessions and fantasies of Idan Hayosh. It is his work that I write about here. I would not have met him without Kathrin Oberrauch and everyone at the residency in Eppan, South Tyrol. I thank all of them for that.

I thank Genia, all the time, for all sorts of things that cannot be put into words, and for constantly encouraging me to write this book.

Introduction

Death hit and I lost my job, all the jobs and death were lost. Even when you ask the mountains, all the languages of mountains, you do not receive a pension or a portion of their growth. Once, while learning Swedish, my teacher asked me where new words come from. I felt I could not seriously say, 'From you, my teacher.' We were thousands of years too late for that, unrobed, and out of the sandy training ground.

So I looked out the window. She followed my eyes, through the screen in our online classroom, up to the sky, then looked at me questioningly. We laughed, almost indistinguishable from people laughing. We believed in something universal.

All our lives, we were brought up on the conviction of the global market. I was pulled out of class, with all the other children, and taken to the main hall, in my first year of secondary school. The head teacher—her square and German body, which I believed to be necessarily connected for years afterwards—climbed on stage and told us all to sit. 'We have gone to war with Iraq,' she said.

And at the same time, Tony Blair wanted to pull down all the council estates, because they were filled with crime and a lack of social drive. Anything that existed in social housing quarters was what the quarters were 'ridden' with. The invisible expansion of Westminster moved into our history of housing, the places where our ancestors had created the rolling myth of us. And the invisible expansion of London and Washington, DC, moved, less invisibly, as bomber jets into the Levant, over racialized territory, smashing up the ground and murdering for the global balance of the market.

My uncle was one of the White bodies carried into war. He watched Brown bodies through a digital telescope, marking himself as central through the definition of whatever is seen by a telescope as *distant*. The looking subject is *here*, in the middle, as the cause. The observed thing is *over there*, tele.

I was one of the tiny White bodies who believed in the universal reach of the Good British Market. My mum told me that those Iraqis treated women badly. Others added an important possessive pronoun: 'They treat *their* women badly.'

I embraced my mum, my three sisters, my sexy Barbie doll. I would *never* treat *my* women badly.

And look what I've become. Hero macho-feminist, doing chin-ups on white birch trees in my Swedish utopia, my countryside Dalarna life, beside my long and chiselled Swedish wife. A saviour of the sensitive sex, unlike those Iraqis who my Great British Uncle shot, for the Grace of the Globe and its Secular Market.

But then one day the world seemed to close and I lost my job. The expanding, universal promise of Britishness opened into a tiny lie, which for me manifested as a one-bedroom council flat in Elephant and Castle.

The universality of the Universal Market was shunned. Everyone said *stay in, stay local*, like we were some radical fringe housing collective. And what do you do, what on earth can you do, when you wake up and your enemies are repeating your opinions? What can happen when you listen to the radio and the prime minister is denying the false universality of the market's global reach? I felt like *I* was the non-universal thing emerging out of global spreads. I had begun a PhD in Black studies and was researching ways of resisting the global reach of racialization, of the market's slapstick drama in every crevasse of the world. All my studies had led me, after years, to the refusal of universality, to the love of little islands. And now the chancellor of the exchequer agreed with me!

As the lie collapses onto your final can of lager before the bluish glow of an empty bank alert, what you need is foreign friends. My lifelong lady Eugenia contacted her impossibly long list of comrades on the continent.

She has a friend in the Dolomites, in the very north of Italy, who runs an art gallery and residency programme. The friend, Kathrin, said she had recently built a new storage facility for her archive of contemporary art. She needed to move everything there: hundreds of artworks, thousands of books, and to register them all in an online archive. She would pay for us to fly to Italy, rent us a car, and let us live in her flat on what is known as the 'Wine Road', which in the two competing local languages—Italian and German—is either the *La Strada del Vino*, or *Weinstraße*.

Genia spent most of the day at the top of a mountain above Bolzano or Bozen, in the new underground archive, processing information through the online system, looking for publisher and date and author names in thousands of art books. Meanwhile, I drove up and down the curvy mountain road, from the previous storage in Kathrin's home to the new location. I had Bob Dylan's latest album on full volume and constant repeat for 2 months, necking chilly non-alco beer as I drove for 10 hours a day, from the lava-heavy heat of Bolzano to the cool arrival of the mountaintop.

As a believer, a Motenist optimist, a fleshy resource of faith in all the best shit, I have inhabited many utopias, regardless of my surroundings. But none has quite surpassed the utopic summer in South Tyrol. There was an abandoned swimming pool beside a medieval church, among a vineyard halfway up a mountain, where we took wine and pizza and tobacco every evening, unabandoning the abandon of the bluest pool.

We were living with a man who had been Genia's lover years before, and his spinal despair was all that held him upright, his calcified core of misery. He smoked with nonstop fury, and he drove in silence, observing the impossibility of his dreams through thickset sunglasses.

Genia wanted to exercise, so he and I went to the lake. We

drank beer and swam and some children jumped on my glasses, supposedly by accident. I drove home blind, blurry, and Genia and I argued. The ex-man took her somewhere, out to be away from me, and we set up a flowing framework of desire.

The next day at the archives I was overheated and the world was overhung with boozing. I stopped the operation of the endless mountain driving, on the verge of vomiting, and took up some archiving. I picked a book from the enormous pile. It was called *LOVE* and had no words, only pictures of tattoos, mostly of dogs, but on people's skin. It was by an Israeli artist called Idan Hayosh.

I felt myocardial electricity fizz me into lovish full life, and I had to write about it:

LOVE, by Idan Hayosh and Corina Künzli

What's love but a mark on the skin? What hates more than the pain of being skin-marked? When a landslide slips on the side of a mountain, the colour doesn't run. It intensifies. The painful stain of motion and rhythm brings the colour *out*, sharper. Nothing is pushed in or subdued by the pain of sweeping over. Landslides are not tattoos. Fair enough. And mountains aren't like skin. I get the feeling Idan Hayosh would hate such a sentimental comparison. But tattoos of puppies are like porn. The performative reproduction that reproduces not reproduction itself but rather the aesthetics of reproduction, that's puppies and porn, *baby*. A pet dog is always already reproduced only as an aesthetic accumulator of cultural value that has been reproduced in order to carry cultural value to the owner. Look how fucking cool I am—I have a dog. And porn—which is the most immediate policy of *LOVE* in San Fran's ubiquitous brand of post-Marxist techno-capitalism that we brutally pseudo-exist inside—lovingly reproduces the cultural value of sex as a purely abstract aesthetics of reproduction. Fucking (as a disguise for labouring) on screen is the same as catching a fish at the fair, shooting the middle of the target or getting a Nobel Prize in quantum mechanics. The reproductive abstraction of reproductive aesthetics. Porn and tattooed puppies are loving reproductions, and all that *LOVE* means in this world is the *LOVE* of capital, the private *LOVE* of branding that puppy into my skin, of investing in the next series of cock-pump advertising and Feminist™ hashtags that reproduce the melting labour time of billionaire culture-porn-puppies in private jets. Eczema itching? Idan and Corina intensify the colour in a landslide of puppy *LOVE*. If Idan gets me a tattoo of a private jet with its own tattoo of me naked on its rock-hard and waxed wings, I'll be the happiest porn puppy alive. *I LOVE IT.*

I was surrounded by mountains and by puppy love, and by Genia who is a polyglot mountain to my silent life in the flatlands, and surrounded by friends who take me out for pizza and beer, and by lakes where fish wink at me as I cast a splint of burnt skin into cracking gleams of lakelight, and by books whose authors paint forest scenes for the fantasies of global reason that insult my little hill-dreams, and by magic.

I posted the paragraph on Instagram and mentioned the account that seemed like it might be Idan Hayosh, @idi_thrice_ removed. He responded a while later with a red love heart.

And then nothing happened.

I re-started a PhD I had barely begun, but this time in the Humanities School at Brighton University, and spent the first few months applying for funding, while working as a welfare manager at another university. I had an argument with the Humanities School and moved to the School of Architecture, finding new supervisors.

I tried to go to Brighton once and my bicycle fell apart on the train, which I understood as divine intervention. I never went back to Brighton.

I was not given funding, not even given a single interview. Another lockdown came, then another. Genia and I decided we wanted our own little puppies to love, human ones, and we wanted to make them in Sweden, where Genia is from. So we moved to Sweden. All our work was online anyway so it made little difference to our schedule.

I started applying to Swedish universities to start my PhD again but with funding this time. Months of Hollywood-level suspense followed and then I got 5 years of full-time PhD funding at Uppsala University, in the English department, which also got me a visa to stay in Sweden permanently.

I had recently finished writing an academic book— *Building Black: Towards Antiracist Architecture*—after its final stage of peer review. The final version was sent off, to sit in the publisher's inbox for months until all the other attendant operations made it ready for publication.

I hated the long waits of writing, the months for anyone to respond, the years between finishing the book and it coming out. When I finished *Building Black*, I was waiting for two collections of my poetry to come out, with different publishers. The first I had finished over 2 years beforehand, and the other a year and a half. A fading bulb of lust for publication was building up inside me.

I was getting bored of work, of dealing with every student's daily disappointment, and of waiting for books to be published, so I broke out sideways into a tunnel, a weird tunnel where all the fish are always dead. Meanwhile, fish are everywhere, on Swedish menus and in the heights of my pleasure as I wrote this book. I was in a hole, forbidden, turned into everything I didn't want to do, like the Preacher says:

If the spirit of the ruler rise up against thee, leave not thy place; for yielding pacifieth great offenses.

There is an evil which I have seen under the sun, as an error which proceedeth from the ruler:

Folly is set in great dignity, and the rich sit in low place.

I have seen servants upon horses, and princes walking as servants upon the earth.

He that diggeth a pit shall fall into it; and whoso breaketh an hedge, a serpent shall bite him (King James Version: Ecclesiastes, 10:4-8).

Writers should write, leaving not our place.

The tunnel opened into the Dolomites, in many languages. Idan was there. He was surrounded by fish in a lake as clear as lakewater, fish as beautiful as fish, and everything was generosity of spirit.

Cast thy bread upon the waters; for thou shalt find it after many days.

Give a portion to seven, and also to eight; for thou knowest not what evil shall be upon the earth.

If the clouds be full of rain, they empty themselves upon the earth: and if the tree fall toward the south, or toward the north, in the place where the tree falleth, there it shall be (KJV: Ecclesiastes, 11:1-3).

I had the most intense dream of my life on the sofa in our flat. I was in the Monticolo/Montiggl lake, surrounded by mountains and dark green pine, black poplars and oak. A huge fish approached me, slow and careless, and spoke to me in Hebrew. I understood Hebrew. We were two aquatic Israelites, alive forever in cool mountain water.

My psychoanalyst understood this fish to be my fiancée, Genia, who is also a psychoanalyst. But I was unsure, unsatisfied with the lack of fish in her response.

I could feel the friendly offering of its scales, and the generosity of its need to give me a new book. It was punching through little scales of sustenance to me, and in the water I was sustained.

The fish was always around me as I was swimming, even if I couldn't see it in the greenish waters. I knew it was probably just keeping some laky snake away from me, or guiding windy waves to other shores. I was as safe as it was possible to be.

And then, in the dream, Genia said that we have to move to the sea, to somewhere near Gävle, on the Baltic coast of Sweden. I had to leave the fish behind, the companion to everything, the scale clogging up the tunnel with its fat and watery life.

We got to some miserable seaside town and I went swimming. The water, being Swedish, was freezing, and all the fish sought to hurt me. They knew what I had been up to with the biggest and best fish in Monticolo, in the warm and greasy beauty of the Dolomites, thick like oil and bitterly fresh like rocky salt and zested lemon. These Baltic fish could feel my ego, its bloated past of pleasure, and they hated me.

How long until a fisherwoman, cruising her fiberglass sails over Monticolo, would kill my fish and photograph the scene?

I searched online for Idan Hayosh, and found his Instagram account. Hundreds of fish were photographed slaughtered, held up by women in bikinis, proudly protected from the water on yachts. Nothing had ever meant so much to me.

I was in love with it all. Like anyone in love, I started writing about fish and an artist I had briefly connected with on Instagram.

I scrolled through his account endlessly, while pretending to work. Idan's Instagram account is called The Institute of Semi-Interesting Maritime Images, Etc., and features hundreds of photographs of fisherwomen holding dead fish. Almost all of the photos are taken on yachts, and not one is taken by the woman in the photograph. There is always an invisible observer who mediates the way of seeing of the picture. In just a few of the scenes, large fish like sharks or aquatic mammals like whales have incidentally washed up on a beach, and a woman is posing — for some reason — beside the corpse. But in almost all of the photos, the fish has been caught and killed, and a woman, on a yacht and in a bikini, is holding up its corpse, proudly smiling for the camera.

These killing scenes are clearly sexualized. Idan took many of the photographs from the account of a fisherman and photographer in Florida's Key West called Hunter Ledbetter, who reveals the scenes' gendered way of looking. He boasts about his double-catch on Instagram. The (fisher)woman has caught a fish, while the (photographer)man has caught both woman and fish.

I started talking about this with Genia, about the bizarre and deadly scenes. She wondered about the status of the trophy. Trophy hunting, trophy wives. The distinctions that cut the violence of imagery was spread wide in these shots. The more we spoke about it, the more there was to say.

Idan writes short texts beside the images. The stories seem to have nothing to do with the images, but as I spent my days increasingly scrolling through them, they became intimately united. The stories follow a first-person character who spends a lot of time at home and occasionally walks around the city. He often loses his girlfriend — sometimes called his 'wife' in the stories — and his credit card. He runs out of money, and is confused by the economic operations of contemporary life. In one of the texts, he phones the bank and asks them to refill his account because it is empty. They tell him that it doesn't work like that. He is stunned, incredulous. He has to get a job, they tell him. He laughs and hangs up the phone.

Over many evenings, Genia and I went through the infinite links: between texts and images, between gendered bodies and caught animals, between the sea and the land, between yachts and Instagram, between photographers and hunters, between artists and writers.

But, of course, Genia has her own life, her days already stacked with meaning, so I had to hold the growing project somewhere else, in some other kind of lovespace.

When it was -20 degrees in Sweden, which seemed crucially significant, I wrote to Idan Hayosh. Genia was an art writer before she trained as a psychotherapist, so she had worked with Kathrin a few times in South Tyrol, at the gallery. Because of that, she knew Idan already. I wrote to him, mentioning the connection through Genia. And then I leapt out of silence with a proposition for a book. He responded almost immediately.

hey Elliot, thanks, i read your text about LOVE a while back, and loved it :) making something about the 'institute' sounds great. i am curious to hear more. give my love to Genia

The triple workings of love—his love of my loving work on his book *LOVE*—was too much to bear, with the love of Genia. I am a little box of excitement-charge, a spilling-over-node of ecstasy, and if you say love three times I burst, and I'll write a book about you.

I tried to hold in the writing for a while, but I was tightly coiled with anticipation. If I held it in, I would establish a crater and a lake would be formed. The geological force of my joy.

Meanwhile, Idan Hayosh carried on his life in Essen, a city surrounded by other cities in the north west of Germany. He lives there with his partner, Friederike, for whom he began the Instagram account. He explains his life to me in an email.

born in israel, grew up in raanana (small town next to tel aviv. 7 min drive to the beach, a bit like brighton, but with more posh folks).

after the army (3 years mandatory in israel. i was in

combat infantry, which means that nowadays i got chronic back pain), at the age of 23, i moved to amsterdam to study art. then 3 years later i started masters in enschede (NL), but quickly decided to quit and just 'be an artist'. i.e: rent a studio and make work. 5 years nothing happend, i was part of the amsterdam underground experimental scene of the 2000s, mostly concerned with installations, that eminate sound/noise, and as part of a scene, i was getting inspired by the crazy great artists of the decade. a bit like what was going around cafe OTO in london back in the day, only 100 fold, and massive scale works. then after 5 years, everything happened.

i make large scale sound installations, very loud, very dangerous (genia can attest to that), and that's about it.

all the works i make are based on photos i collect. i take the photo, trace its composition, or the outline of its content, and then revive it, using my own set of objects, mechanics and materials, then show it to folks. and drink the beer.

when i met friederike, at an opening (in germany, where i moved to after 10 years in holland), and asked for her e-mail adress, she said she's on instagram and that we should talk there. so i joined instagram, that was a couple of years ago. and since then, i post stuff to try to impress her :) she is a linguist, so i had to start 'writing' stuff for the first time in my life, to fit her interest. we are together since then and she did not leave, so i guess it works!

so those collections, posts, and text, for me, are a life thing. i do not see an artistic quality in it, as i am so immersed in my own 3 dimensional practice. i get it that people do see quality, and are affected by it, but i don't. for me they are leftovers from an obsession of collecting, that are a layout of decorations to make people laugh (or to make my girlfriend stay).

We write to each other, in long and unstructured confessions, giving more and more to the other as it begins to emerge that one of us is really going to write a book about the other, and both our girlfriends stay. He tells me to call him 'Idi', which is what his friends call him, so I write a whole book addressed to Idi. Our love is locked into the practice of writing, the sociality of sound and sight that forms months of a kind of scripted embrace between Essen and Stockholm, and then to Falun, where Genia and I moved when she got a better job there.

Without a title yet, I wrote the book like prayer, like seraphic dedication to all my forms of love. To Genia and her work as a psychotherapist and psychoanalytic theorist. To Fred Moten, my dream and patron saint in the undercommon world of Black studies. To Idan and his heavy sounds, his constant distortion, his humour and his imagery that runs across a strange flat space outside and beyond liberal ethics, with a demeanour that is impossible to understand.

I thought about all the yachts in Key West at the bottom of Florida, where I've never been and I'll never go, about Bob Dylan's love of Key West, his 10-minute ritual feast of gargling in minor Florida keys, and I thought about islands, about my love and her smell which took me all the way to the end of a book about islands.

Come with me from Lebanon, my spouse, with me from Lebanon: look from the top of Amana, from the top of Shenir and Hermon, from the lions' den, from the mountains of the leopards.

...Thy lips, O my spouse, drop as the honeycomb: honey and milk are under thy tongue; and the smell of thy garments is like the smell of Lebanon.

A garden enclosed is my sister, my spouse; a spring shut up, a fountain sealed (KJV: Song of Songs, 4:8-12).

I put together a few ideas, maybe ten pages of writing, laid alongside Idan's images from Instagram and the stories that accompany them. I proposed a collaboration, a way of writing this book together, somehow between Sweden and Germany. He responded, and handed over control of the book to me, politely refusing my offer of collaboration.

Instead, I decided to write the book in the form of a letter to Idi, set in the Institute of Maritime Images, Etc. What happened next is *The Instagram Archipelago*.

Throughout the book, I talk about lots of different things, in these sliced and splattered conversations with Idi. I talk about his Instagram account, and its bizarre images of fisherwomen, the scene of the kill repeated so many times that it becomes banal, becomes entertaining even. The images in this book — in the section *Idan Hayosh's Institute of Maritime Images, Etc.*, which comes after the main text — are not actually those on his Instagram account. Because of Instagram image quality and copyright laws, I have had to replace his archive of fisherwomen with similar stock images. The stock images, being stock, are nowhere near as shocking or personal as the images Idi has collected online, but they show more or less the same thing: the kill, the visuality, the frames of seeing and the caught lines of history. But they are prepared, they are staged and over-determined by the requirements of stock sales, so they are not the same. Because of that, I have put only a brief selection of them in this book. For the full hit, the sharp zest of the multi-layered killing scene, you have to visit the Instagram account itself.

It's important to note that when I refer to specific images in the text, which I refer to by the date Idi posted them on Instagram, I am referring to the ones on his account, not the ones in this book.

Throughout all of the imaged conversions with Idi, the passages of study and of love that fill this book, there is one unifying proposition, which I try to develop in more academic and more architectural ways in my book *Building Black*, and in various essays.

The proposition really comes out of a disappointment with the conviction of atheist liberalism. The liberal (and atheist) mode attempts to universalize a particular way of seeing the world, and treats that universalization as a gesture of benevolent inclusion. The liberal way of seeing sees parts of the world as wrong, and it attempts to turn them into the *right way* of atheist liberalism. It is an expansive way of knowing the world, folding all of life into a single ethical proposition. This ethical proposition of atheist liberalism is, in its own logic, unquestionably right. For liberal atheists, it is *impossible* that anything divine or godly could exist; and for atheist liberals, closed borders, secluded and independent cultures, prescribed traditions and rituals, and the refusal of production are *totally unfeasible.*

Within most religious, pantheist, or agnostic belief systems, however, belief in God/gods is not absolute. There always exists the possibility that there is no god, or that there is another god, an unknown kind of god.

In the area of contemporary philosophy called Black radicalism, moreover, there is a fundamental belief in people's ability to develop and build their own traditions and rituals, and a respect for those independent rituals that might be unknowable to a dominant logic. Black radicals would not propose teaching different traditions in a single school system, for example, because then all the independent non-hegemonic traditions taught in schools become subsumed inside the dominant logic that orders the curriculum and the central way of knowing the world.

Instead, Black radicals would say that it is more radical— and therefore more ethical—to have different schools for people with different traditions, in order for their tradition, and their particular way of knowing the world, to be maintained, and to be discussed, studied, and developed by the practitioners of that tradition itself.

The idea of Black radicalism is to resist the urge to universalization and its necessary subsumption of different and divergent cultures. And the idea of agnosticism or a doubtful position within religion is to recognize and respect the meaning of traditions themselves; to give time and study to the observation and practice of rituals, which create the meaning of cultural groups, without the totalizing and self-convinced claims of atheism, and without the universalization of liberalism.

I call this *Black island thinking*. The *Black* in *Black island thinking* is taken from Black studies, which is also called the Black radical tradition.

I try to make a proposition for *Black island thinking* principally through a reading of Idan's images from his Instagram account, but I also follow many paths into other cultural phenomena. In this book I talk about such things as contemporary Black cinema, American fishing blogs, early colonial maps of the USA, the actor Emma Watson, the model Emily Ratajkowski, the philosopher Tiffany Lethabo King and her idea of Black shoals, Japanese bathrooms, Chance the Rapper and his hidden Judaism, the structure of Jewish belief systems, Jesus Christ and Saint Peter, John Berger and the zoos he visits, Nina Simone's nuclear weaponry, and Aristotle's breezy robe as he strokes fish on Lesbos.

What I try to make clear either by celebrating or criticizing — or both — each of these and many more scenes is that their *violence* comes from any attempt to universalize themselves. As soon as an ethical proposition or act attempts to claim universal validity, and to establish a homogeneous world in which it is itself the ideal of reason, then it becomes violent and unsustainable. It is unsustainable in the sense that it literally stops the possibility of its own existence by its own violence, which is constantly disrupting the logic that allows it to exist.

What I propose instead is a cultural logic that celebrates the differences of non-universal ways of thinking.

In Lena Waithe and Melina Matsoukas's 2019 film *Queen & Slim*, for example, the two eponymous protagonists have their own logic among themselves, which is not concerned with the universalized logic of the racist police. The two characters want to go to Cuba, by first driving south through the USA and then by catching a plane from Florida. Outside of their own little island of internal thinking, there is a global logic of police surveillance that has already caught and killed this couple. The existence of the police already means capture and death for the subjects it exists to police: Black subjects; racialized subjects; juridical and ontological anti-subjects.

So, Queen and Slim are not concerned with the police's logic. That universalized code already signifies their own death, so they ignore it and reduce their world to the internal meaning of their own little island, their own language that the police cannot understand. In the film this is portrayed literally, as the characters often speak to each other without opening their mouths or making any sound.

In *Queen & Slim*, a Black island of resistance is successfully formed against the universalizing reach of a violent, hegemonic logic. The characters are murdered by police officers in the final scene, but their island logic of internal difference survives, and the threat they pose to the neat global reach of the police remains despite their deaths.

The islands have their own way of knowing, each island with its own internal system. They function against and without the expansive form of the sea, the sea that is always expanding into the dry and warm social life of land. The sea is the universalizing force, the police, the empire, the nation-state as a logic of subsumption. The island, meanwhile, holds its own internal language, and that little island language allows one island to speak to others, so all the islands understand a certain kind of difference that cannot be caught by the sea.

It is that kind of island of resistance that I seek in *The Instagram Archipelago*.

One difficult question silently performed in this book is whether I—as a White man—am enacting an atheist liberal mode of writing by universalizing my Whiteness into the study of Black radicalism. Ultimately, Black radicalism is a tradition for Black people, for the specific and independent cultures of Blacks and the meaning of Blackness. By writing another book of Black study, while being White, I am inevitably subsuming a part of Black studies into my White way of knowing the world.

I confront this difficulty at various sections in the book, but still I have no final answer or definitive excuse for my involvement.

This is a book about an Instagram account that is made of lots of second-hand images of women in bikinis holding dead fish. It is also about the politics and poetics of visuality, about the violence of ways of seeing, about the mechanisms of sight that this long era of global expansion is based on. It is about gender, too, and race. It is about the ways in which forms of human life are gendered and racialized through complex streams of invisible and hypervisible violences over centuries. It is also about bikinis, and the way clothing codes the body within. It is about art, too, and the productions that provide or fail to provide openings into other ways of thinking. It is about Black studies, the radical contemporary school of thinking that is always escaping from presupposed forms, the study group that I am obsessed with. It is about Black women scholars, about discussing what Black women say in academia and literature not necessarily *because* they are Black women but because the Black women quoted and engaged with in this book have a lot to say, and because so few texts from outside the practice of Black studies are concerned with their works. This book is about the land and the sea, and about a certain form of internal and undercommon radicalism that I call 'Black island thinking'. It is, largely, about islands. About islands of thinking, and islands of existing otherwise, and islands where no one who writes the canonical texts will go. It is about islands that I don't know how to get to, or how to find. It is about islands that I love to think of, to study with. It is about the way the sea is always expanding, with and as global empires, as neoliberal capitalism, and how these oppressive movements attempt to turn everything into themselves, and about how islands resist that expansion, that homogenization. It is about Judaism, about Jews, about Israel, about the Torah, about prayer and about dance and about music. It is about the peculiar site of Instagram, and about the ways in which specific cultural productions can open paths towards understanding the fundamental mechanisms of modernity that produce racialized and gendered lives, and open other ways of understanding life and ourselves and the world. It is about those little islands of possibility, about the optimism of radical life on islands that refuse to become the sea. It is about Idan Hayosh, about the noisy fantasies of Idi. And it is about the lives of dead fish.

Choking on Guys and Gills

I have maps all over my body that tell you who I am, Idi, where I'm from, what I'm doing here. I read your epidermis like a dirty novel, like shelf-life. You're not scaly, and neither am I.

We are equally covered in historical lines that lead the viewer to a scene of violence, a violating scene of initiation. Mine and yours are connected. That's why I speak in long letters to you, instead of going fishing on the long magnetic sea.

I have maps all over my body. The only thing my body knows is holding maps up, signifying histories that lead to me. If I went fishing, I could take photographs of women in bikinis, but they'd already know the result, because the lines are etched all over me.

No one is filming us here, at the Institute of Maritime Images, Etc. No one knows where we are going, but we are tracked by the markings in our skin.

In the first post in the Institution, *October 17, 2018*, Idi, you are taken away by famous stars to sparkling parties and stuff. You realize soon afterwards, however, that it was a linguistic problem all along: they were 'just STARS in my eyes from the pain' of having cut yourself while shaving. The absence of a recorded life is the reason for your lostness. You lose yourself in the inability to recognize people by their appearance on screens. Who are you if you were never filmed, if your skin wasn't written into my constituting cartography?

No one, Idi.

* * *

Australian philosopher Elizabeth Grosz sees no difference between the body and its technological prosthetics.[1] There was never a pure body in a mythical time before technology,

19

and then these additions came along. The *body* itself only has meaning as an apparatus constituted *with* technology; or rather, what *humanity* means is the conflation of body and technology, and they are necessarily inseparable.

'If it exists at all (and it is no longer clear to me that it does),' Grosz says, 'the biological body exists for the subject only through the mediation of a series of images or representations of the body and its capacities for movement and action.'[2] The *body* is a machine through which subjectivity experiences the world, which can also be used as a mediating point for other embodied experiences: driving through the body of a car, using the car's spatial limits, for example.

The merged constitution of body and subjectivity is the condition for the use of the world, as Grosz says. Anything humans can consider using, from hitting stuff with sharpened rocks to the extraction of fossil fuels, becomes a constituting part of the mediation that occurs as the humans' world. It is, ultimately, a usable world, and that begins at the point of subjectivity's use of the body.

Winner of Athens' Top Toga Model 349 BCE, Aristotle thinks of the body as necessarily already having a use, which he calls *ergon* — each *man*'s duty. The carpenter's wood-carving body *is* the use of the carpenter, and that is how carpenters are born, which is revealed constantly through the materialization of wooden objects from the carpenter's studio. If you keep making chairs, then you know you were born to be a carpenter. Or as the Philosopher-model puts it, 'for the function of a lyre-player is to play the lyre, and that of a good lyre-player is to do so well'.[3]

For Aristotle, a person's *ergon*/duty is that person's technology: the thing you can do is what you were born to do, and that is how you use the world. Use is the chains in which the human is caught — the body must be used, and it must be used to use the world. Use can never stop. The only thing the world can never be to humans is useless. Anything useless is destroyed or consumed, and something that can be used replaces it. That's the extent of humans' faith in Aristotle.

The other thing for Aristotle, as he writes in his *Nicomachean Ethics*, is that there are no stages of activity—doing things is not given in levels, or in degrees of importance: activity itself is the duty of man, any activity, as long as it is *his duty*. As he writes, 'if the function of man is an activity of soul which follows or implies a rational principle...human good turns out to be activity of soul exhibiting excellence'. [4] Just do what you do, whether you do it well or not, as long as you are *doing*.

In our era's global capitalist economy, the command to *use* becomes the profit-productive use of the body. The human must use the body to create and circulate profit. The body becomes a profit-productive category itself. American cultural theorist Grace Kyungwon Hong writes of the current phase of neoliberal capitalism, 'in which the value of speculative capital far outweighs that of productive capital, race, gender, and sexuality are categories created by the process of turning *existence itself* into forms usable for speculative capital, as sheer surplus'. [5] The racialized body's existence is itself a function of capitalism's ultimate aim: the constant circulation of capital. Turning the body into categories allows profit to be circulated at various levels, in a more complex and violent mode of qualified use than Aristotle could even imagine.

The maps marked in the skin and organs of human bodies are the codes of human value. Mid-twentieth-century east Asian migration to the USA allowed the global hegemon to inflect its neo-colonial wars in Korea and Vietnam with the image of liberal charity, *saving* Asians from the evil of communism. US prisons full of Black people are a method of turning a once-industrial labour force into the raw material of surplus, working for free in cages. [6] And, like Italian scholar Silvia Federici says, the feminization of half the human population has always been a way of keeping men in the constant production of profit: 'women' make *men*, 'men' make *profit*.[7]

Mapping the world is a process of constructing a certain kind of subjectivity that imagines the possibility of a body moving through the world—certain bodies, given centrality in the map and the process of map-making, can easily transfer themselves from place to place, while other bodies are defined by trappedness.

The history of the map itself already opens the meaning of who can move and who cannot: the global map, as we tell ourselves its mythical foundation story, was created by White European Christian men who sailed around the oceans and took note of what they saw. The map is a practice of *inscription*, of writing down what European men see. What the map *means* is also the movement of White men, like me, Idi. I can move, you know, all over the globe, like an oily vessel on spreading water.

In the fifteenth century, when these men started mapping the earth and calling it the singular World, cartography was a form of global surveillance that seemed to replace the ubiquitous eye of God with the rationality of the map: some people lived in torrid lands, and torrid bodies, and they were irrational and enslavable; others lived in temperate lands, and temperate bodies, and they were rational and profit-productive, able to use slaves to make profit.[8]

These technologies of surveillance are very different now. As Canadian theorist of surveillance Simone Brown discusses, the greater fear than being constantly observed in the semantics of social media is *not* being observed. We fear our posts being unread, terrified of the realization that in fact no one is interested in watching us.[9] Fugitivity was the method of the enslaved escapee. They fled into unobservable land, away from the bordered territory of the masters. They set up *quilombos* and other fugitive communities.

Now, every single movement is already wrapped into the

logic of profit-reproduction. The movements of the global economy no longer need to focus on human bodies, since we are already totally convinced of its plan. We dominate ourselves, reproducing tradability in our every thought.

The problem with the prosthetic subjectivity of cartography — with these maps all over our bodies, and their social meaning — is not that it is morally wrong. As Grosz says,

(My objections to pornography are not that it is morally wrong or should be banned but that it is boring and ritualistic, and needs to be made relevant to and pleasurable for women.) Virtual spaces run the probability of only ever becoming another space that men colonize in the name of a generic humanity but that serves only their particular interests.[10]

The cartography of the body creates a map that is already inscribed as the meaning of the body, and it is nonnegotiably male, heterosexual, White, abled-bodied, and Euro-American. That is the problem of the body's internal maps. They signify only one thing: the profit-productive categories of race, gender, sexuality, and their use in and as the global economy, which is also called the Sea.

* * *

The only way of doing philosophy with any kind of meaningful ethics, I think, is to take French philosopher Simone Weil's route: How can everyone stop being hungry? and then to immediately insert into that the internal question: Can we live with ourselves, given that people *are* hungry and we are doing philosophy?

Can we really bear to be ourselves? Is this kind of subjectivity endurable? You spend 7 percent of your entire savings at the races, Idi, and yet you go on — in *February 15, 2021* — spending the next season building boxes full of dreams that imagine a world in which 'girlfriend' does not equal 'angry and perplexing challenge', as it does in our own misogynist economy.

Legendary French philosopher Simone de Beauvoir said that the main task of philosophy was not to make people happy or stop them being hungry, but to find the meaning of existence. Simone Weil, her mystical challenger, responded, *you've obviously never been hungry then.*[11]

If you haven't been hungry, you don't approach life as the task of keeping yourself away from hunger. If you haven't had to endure hard labour, you don't plan your life according to its distance from hard labour. If you haven't been in prison, you don't qualify the meaning of openable doors and private keys.

If you're a man and you haven't been fishing, then you've probably never taken a photograph of a woman in a bikini holding a dead fish, blood running down her balded skin.

I haven't been fishing, Idi. But once, when I was 11, I went down to the river with my friend Patch. His dad was into fishing and we took his gear, his macho-paternal tackle. We walked along the river until we made it out of town, and then we sat down and dipped the pole in the brown water.

We talked about the girls at school, who were called 'girls' then. Now they're all grown up and they have two options: women, or Fishing Girls. They can't be both and they can't be neither. Unless they ask the Photographer, but He works in mysterious ways.

Years and years passed and then the string moved. It tugged us toward it. Something had caught our time and ended its infinity. We bounced up from the muddy verge and were frightened right back into childhood. Tugging too early for our time. Learning, slowly, how to tug together.

The fish came up and it was exactly what I suspected a fish would look like. Because it was short, bald, quiet, and seemed disappointed and angry at my position as its inevitable murderer. I called it 'Dad', but it didn't answer to the name.

First, we thought it didn't answer because it was dead. We put it in a plastic bag and unhooked its mouth from the rod. We blamed the fish itself for biting the hook, but it seemed to blame us, since we put the hook in the water where fish live.

We walked all the way back to Patch's house and just when we were about to go in, the plastic bag started wriggling. We screamed and ran inside. I dropped the bag on the kitchen counter and Patch grabbed a knife. No one else was home. He looked at me, and the fish inside a plastic bag, and me again.

Plastic bags, I really do believe, are quite useful when you want to hold numerous small things at the same time in only one hand. They don't hold much fish blood, though. I promise you this, Idi; I don't care who you are or where you're from: your bag won't hold a fish's worth of blood. It'll go everywhere if you cut its head off.

Patch cut its head off. There was none of the romance that videogames had taught me about murder. Nothing cool happened afterwards. No one even asked us about it. There was no next level to progress to. There was just ourselves, alone with a dead fish, wiping up blood inside a plastic bag.

So I suppose, Idi, I have been fishing. But maybe fishing should just be called murdering.

* * *

I've never eaten meat, not one bite in my life, but I killed a fish repeatedly. There's no way you could have known that, Idi, until I told you. No way you ever could have tasted the vegetable stew of my simmering lifetime, and the noiseless fantasies of my urge to kill.

* * *

At the Institute of Maritime Images, Etc., Idi, your (unnamed) girlfriend leaves you hundreds of times. She reappears again, her returning vessel floating into view. She is framed inside an act of disappearance that never ends, that can never be complete.

In *November 1, 2019*, your girlfriend is adamant that she does not need you to meet her at the airport when her flight arrives. You take her at her word. Language for you is universal: *no* means *no*, so you don't go to the airport.

Your girlfriend, however, 'said that it's 2019 and that her generation is so random, and flimsy, and shallow, that the word NO, as well as the word YES, is actually a suggestive term and not a decisive decision, because everybody is changing their minds all the time, and cannot commit on some NO's or YES's in their lives'.

Language has no universal proclamations for her. Inside the frame of womanhood, the meaning of language is different. Something about this relationship between gender and language seems to define the fact that she is the girlfriend, the object of the story. She is not narrating, not constructing the frame the viewer sees.

Confused and deserted by your girlfriend, Idi, you go to the library to inform them that they need to update the definition of 'yes' and 'no'. They have misinformed you of something, convincing you that meaning is universally homogeneous. You thought 'yes' always meant affirmation and 'no' was always negation. But it turns out the meaning was only universal *for you*.

And *for you* also means *for the fact that you are a man*.

Idi, as the narrator, creates the narrative frame. You place the borders of the story around the object, and that area becomes the scene. Idi is the cartographer, inscribing lines of embodied meaning in the space of the narrative world, birthing the body of Woman as a spotlighted location within the World of Men.

Your girlfriend is in the (non-)place that American writer

Anne Boyer calls 'the girls' city':

> The girls' city does not exist. Girls are born into a no place in particular that is owned by men; it matters little where or how; they die there in the nothing as they die everywhere that has men; it matters not where, nor how. They have never had a city of their own; the girls have no ruins; they have no histories to forget; there is no language whose words they must unlearn; the girls have no orations trailing off their lips; the girls have no official records to burn: they have no location but the nothing location of everywhere that is with the men.[12]

You place your girlfriend in the ruins of your own tradition. This is not so much a limitation for *her* understanding of the scene or the narrative, since it was never intended for her anyway. It is rather, I think, a false universalization of the meaning of ruins in Idi's World of Men.

Those ruins were particular to us, Idi, to the hunters with all our fishing tackle, our machogendered armoury, and as that they were fine. But in the narratives, in the posts sustained by the architecture of Instagram, these gendered nuclear ruins become universalized, expanding to an impossibly inflated size.

How big's your ruin, Idi? Send a pic. A disappearing slice of the macho-image machine.

This is what Tobago-born Canadian writer M. NourbeSe Philip says about Black and Indigenous theatre. 'Can you ever have a valid completion of a work by an audience that is a stranger to the traditions that underpin the work?'[13] Her answer, of course, is *not really*, so why am I reading her? I will never understand, never know the workings of her Black, Caribbean, and Woman tradition, but my phallic authority quotes her anyway, universalizing the reach of my writing Sea.

I am *eating the energy* of M. NourbeSe Philip in order to

expand the territory of my own writing. I think this becomes clearer throughout these words exchanged at the Institute of Maritime Images, Etc., because I use more and more of the energy, until I am everywhere, like the sea, Idi. But Philip has a way of talking that is inaccessible to me. She has the ability to build shoals in the sea. And your girlfriend, Idi, can push the meaning of 'no' around, distorting the sense of your expansion.

So much of the so-called developing world has been/is being consumed — literally — slipping into the great maw of the West and slipping down its throat to its stomach, there to be digested and transformed into some imitation of the original. And bearing names like 'world music' that separate the product from its source. In such a world, to be indigestible — to have the ability to make consumption difficult — is a quality to be valued.[14]

* * *

Some artists, Idi, are not only called artists. They are called 'female artists' or even 'women artists'. What this means is that, while constructing the artistic meaning within the frame of display, they are also themselves inside the frame.

The *artist* opens a constructed frame and disappears, leaving the receivers of art to make their choices. The *female artist* lingers inside the frame, always synonymous with her production. Everything else she does is an addition to the meaning inside the frame. Of particular importance in the development of this meaning called *female artist* is whether she wears a bikini.

The *female artist*'s artistic frame is a map that guides the viewer to her internal meaning. There is a map on the surface of every production by the *female artist* and it lays out a code of meaning.

We ask ourselves at the gallery if the *female artist* wears a bikini when she is not at the gallery. If she'll wear a bikini *here*, in the Institute itself. If she'll take the bikini off, which I think a man called Patrik Alac is waiting for. These are the kinds of rumours you often hear at the Institute of Maritime Images, Etc., in the World of Men.

We talk about what's under the bikini endlessly. The funny thing is that we know what's there—we already learnt the secret, years ago. We know there are things called *breasts* and *vagina*. But the next layer of the secret is that we don't know what's under *there*. We can all open bikinis by now. We've been doing that for years. One-handed, even. And with the distraction of a boner in swimming trunks.

But we don't know what's under *there*. There are breasts and vagina, but *what are they?*

I can follow the signs on the map that lead me to breasts and vagina, but I don't know what the mapping means.

It feels like men made maps to cohere with the male body—the White, European male body. The entire map of life, all the lines we forge to make meaning in the world, is based on *my body*, Idi; my narcissistic White man's frame. When I try to read the meaning of Blackness, of Womanness, of anything that isn't me, it is necessarily incoherent in the lines of meaning that I have learnt forever.

I use the same maps as people just like me used in the fifteenth century, and they guide me to kitchens, plantations, prisons, and collapsing blocks of social housing.

What I learn from other people who make no sense on global maps is what M. NourbeSe Philip told us, on some other day at the Institute, in our long and calorific conversations: *In such a world, to be indigestible—to have the ability to make consumption difficult—is a quality to be valued.*

Philip crosses lines on the global maps of meaning. She distorts and confuses the signifying function of cartography. She breaks the racializing and gendering code of the system we are stuck inside. She opens gaps in the fabric of the scroll.

* * *

The *female artist* is creative in the sense that her use of the limitations of gender-maps on her skin forces language to signify otherwise. She uses the maps of feminization carved in her skin as a means of distorting the function of universal language, rupturing its universality.

The *female artist*, it seems from this distance, doesn't tolerate the distortion of her position. Instead, she distorts the logic of positionality. She doesn't let other people into her deformed island on the Sea of global map-making. She builds a fortress and spits out of keyhole embrasures. She clogs the throat of the makers of language.

At the Institute, Idi, we reject tolerance. We are anti-liberal. Like Professor Tariq Jazeel says, 'claims to "tolerance" in contemporary multiculture should be regarded with suspicion, for behind the spectre of tolerance is always a tolerating (usually liberal, rational, western) "I", always-already at liberty to suffer the difference of others'.[15] We do not tolerate anything, politely nodding at the staged scene of difference, while running our fingers along the lines of our body-maps. We do not merrily wave at the emblems of passing difference. No, Idi. We batter ourselves over the head and tear apart the map, while we learn from the *female artist* how she creates a different language within the cartography of these maps that cover us.

But we won't learn — we hunters will never learn, Idi. And we should never try and practise what the *female artist* tells us. The whole point is that the language she uses is a language specific to herself, to be understood by *female artists* on the island — an island we are not only rejected from, but that we were born to destroy.

By looking at a certain form of life, we code it as a *female artist*.

We turn its creativity into a gendered product of the misogynist economy. Helplessly, endlessly, we just repeat this scene.

So Idi, what we male observers read in the frame of the *female artist* is our projective male cartography. Masculinity is a regulating map that gives directions to the meaning of *looking*; visual semantics are defined by the projectile eyes of men.

This doesn't really mean that the Male Gaze constructs the world, or that the feminized people called 'women' or even 'fishing girls' disappear as autonomous beings within the sights of men. It means, more profoundly, that the function of mapping space is the affirmation of misogyny. The reason for constructing lines of meaning in the world is to strictly delineate what certain kinds of *bodies* and *people* mean. Taking photographs of women fishing is not just an act of taking photographs of women fishing. It is also the making of worlds based on the hunt: the hunt for fish, and the hunt for capturing women in bikinis.

American cultural and art theorist Tiffany Lethabo Kings writes that geography is the project of human-making.[16] The making of the conceptual gridlines of the world is the making of the space in which human life is coordinated and authorized. The 'human' can only be understood by the social coordinates of the body's epidermal maps.

If the women in bikinis on the fishing boats jumped into the ocean, they would still be women in bikinis who belong on fishing boats. The fishing women would only be stuck in the binary conundrum of subaquatic colour: if her skin is light, she is seen from above the water, against the dark ocean, and caught by hungry map-making men; if her skin is dark, she is seen from below, against the light sky, and caught by hungry ocean creatures.

* * *

In his *Life Studies*, American poet Robert Lowell writes about throwing 'cold water' on his parents' 'watery martini pipe dreams at Sunday dinner' by refusing to go with them, instead demanding to stay at his grandparents' house.[17] The watery martini of the bourgeois, domestic dream is familiar. It is a space of wetness, where diseases grow, where mouths stick and suck for satiation. It is a conceptual space of dampening drought; where the dry distance of listening is packed away into the comforting proximity of the baby's mouth that laps up mother's milk. But why does he throw more water at the watery scene?

He wants to remain within the family scene, in the source at the top, the grandparents' embrace, the watering hole, the life-giving machine, but he already has excess water, a pail of it brought from some other scene.

Lowell's parents' life is *haute bourgeois* fantasy, a palatial space of expanding luxury. Their established American pseudo-royal lineage is practised in every word and every movement, extending into and as the territory of the USA—whatever the Lowells do *is America*. These bourgeois American dynasties create a peculiar Americanized tribal system, in which fashion and *the done thing* (linked either to Paris, London, or Milan—and more recently Scandinavia, too) is the mode of conquest. They don't use cars and guns and intimidation, like working-class American tribes; they use tutting and slight gestures of the head. If you do it wrong, you *are wrong*, and that is an offense punishable by relegation to the non-Europeanized space of America. You lose your Parisness, your Milanosity. You're trailer trash, or you're Black; unmortgagable: death by exclusion from death.

Lowell's parents' bourgeois life is an expanding sea that turns everything into itself, not turning things exactly into a *sea*, but turning everything wet, soaked in the unmistakable mark of salty water.

The flooded land does not become known as a sea. It is

flooded land, far inferior to both land and sea. It becomes almost useless, removed from any notion of use by humans.

Lowell's wet dreams rediscover the scene of the expanding sea, its breaking boundaries, the bloated seams just before an imperial puncture. It is going to get everywhere, to turn the entire republic into a feudal property of the post-European gentry. It is wet, soaking wet, like an indifferent sea that simply expands into everything.

It is believed of British history, particularly, that Empire was conducted *on* the sea. The same is believed of the Spanish and Portuguese. But this misunderstands what the sea means. *The Empire is the Sea.*

People from the coasts of Africa and the Caribbean do not swim in the Sea. It is known in these coastal epistemologies what the Sea really means. It means Empire, and it is the mechanism of murderous expansion.

Italian architect and theorist Pier Vittorio Aureli develops the idea of urbanization as a sea that expands as the city, turning the manifold lives of the city into one single aesthetic regime that collapses time into its own form: everything must become urbanized, homogenized into the pattern of urbanity.[18]

Urbanization is a form — a model for structuring space — that *must* constantly expand, moving into non-uniform space and turning it into a part of the dominant form of urbanity. As the Sea turns everything wet, leaving its soggy mark on all land encountered in the necessary expansion of water, urbanization leaves everything categorized by the form of urbanity.

For Aureli, there is a radical possibility in the non-relation of the island. The island that resists becoming the Sea has a language and a mode of its own; it has *survived* history, it has *endured* the constant encroachment of the Sea, and that makes the island a place of real possibility. It does not extend itself out as the world, as the entirety of one global concept. Instead, it remains inwards-focused, formed of its own kind of social practice: the sociality that goes on within the boundaries of the island is a sociality that makes no claim over other social practices.

Empire is the form of anti-sociality—the form of social organization that ends the *social*—that cannot bear to be singular or specific; it must be universal. Everyone inside the British Empire becomes a subject of the Empire, subjected to its universal authority.

The island form of sociality has no such interest. It cares nothing for universalization. In the archipelago, the island has its own way of speaking, and it doesn't want to impose its language on anyone, because its form is already the form of endurance, of surviving the universal Empire of the Sea.

> The concept of the archipelago describes a condition where parts are separated yet united by the common ground of their juxtaposition. In contrast to the integrative apparatus of urbanization, the archipelago envisions the city as the agonistic struggle of parts whose forms are finite and yet, by virtue of their finiteness, are in constant relationship both with each other and with the 'sea' that frames and delimits them. The islands of the archipelago describe the role of architectural form within a space more and more dominated by the 'sea' of urbanization.[19]

The island, though, cannot so easily achieve this liberation from the universalizing form of the Sea. The Sea is always trying to establish its Empire as the World: its mode is what we know as the World.

If the earth was made of islands, there would be no such thing as the World. We would exist within many earths, all understood differently. Instead, we have the Empire of World.

Filipino philosopher Neferti X. M. Tadiar calls this 'City Everywhere', a kind of urban movement that is always in the imperial mode, using aesthetics and technology as bayonets. For Tadiar, it is not so much architecture itself that achieves this imperial model of endless expansion, but rather what this urban mode does to human subjectivity. The form of human life created by City Everywhere — or the expanding Sea of Empire — is one that cannot bear difference; it must subsume itself at every moment within the global, homogeneous practice of the City, which is also the World.

'In a global communicative-biocapitalist economy where circulation itself has become value-productive,' she writes, 'and the channels of conveyance of material, immaterial, human as well as nonhuman content have become the very generative site — the *platforms* — of reconstituted urban life, they *are* the city.'[20] The way we communicate is also the way we trade. Profit-reproduction is indistinguishable from contact, relations, language, and the daily practice of being alive.

Huge motorways, aeroplane routes, internet communication, and the physical transfer of human life through tourism and emigration become the *way of connecting* and the *content* of the City. The means of making links between everywhere, always, is also the content of those links. Our language becomes a global language of connectedness, referring only to its constant expansion. 'In them the form of connection and the substance of content aim to be one and the same,' Tadiar writes.[21]

These communicative technologies — themselves the content of urbanization, alongside its homogenizing architecture — create a frame around all forms of life. The frame designates *visibility* within the city. It is a frame with a lens that allows certain forms of life to be *unseen*. Those life-forms that speak the language of universality, that can communicate in the form and content of the Sea, are allowed to disappear, transferring themselves silently around the World.

They wear things that make them look universal, too: suits, smart dresses, polished shoes, lanyards, combed and gelled hair, and, so importantly, light skin. Aesthetically, this relegates many forms of life to the condition of *visibility*: they cannot slide freely around the World, within its expanding waters, because certain elements of their lives flick a glitch warning in the operation: afros (non-combed and gelled hair), turbans, hijabs (non-visible hair), dark skin, visible disabilities, kitenge.

Being messy or growing out otherwise-conforming White hair, wearing baggy or torn clothes, etc., are not methods of becoming visible in the operations of global movement. The punk aesthetic or the rocker outfit is no longer suspicious. This is just the temporary uniform of the bourgeois, holding onto the irony of non-conformance when the body inside the costume *ontologically signifies* conformance; the White body is invisible, and can freely travel like capital, like flows of investor funds, because regardless of its disguise it was born into the World made for that body to connect to everything.

Non-conformance, I mean, is not chosen. It is a permanent state of certain kinds of lives. These kinds include Black lives, Muslim lives, Arab lives, Brown lives, Jewish lives, disabled lives, and the lives of *female artists*. These lives are lived as *visible* in the optic operation of the urbanizing World.

The Sea expands endlessly, keeping watch over everything, and whatever can be seen will be subsumed. The invisible lives of the White, hetero, property-owning bourgeoisie glide through the optic mechanisms without the slightest barrier, since the purpose of the Sea's expansion is their freedom to move. The invisible lives have access to everything; they can enter anywhere, never seen, just anonymous tokens of a White heritage that allowed them the key of universality. 'This is the investor fantasy of "world class": a total, enveloping media-cosm in which "access" is the keyword,' as Tadiar writes, 'the defining feature of a *keyed world*.'[22]

Islands of Blackness, of Muslimness, of Arabness, of Jewishness, of Brownness, of gendered womanness stand above the eclipsing wetness of the ampliative Sea, mounds of enduring resistance in the soaking archipelago.

The islands construct a certain image on their enduring shores, manipulating the flow of the tidal Sea. It washes in closer when the island seems to be distracted or giving up its hypervisibility. To froth the homogeneity of the Sea and storm the archipelago's rising tide, Aureli proposes a form of architecture that is explicitly and solely attendant to its islandness. Aureli wants to build a city that stops at its own borders, in which every building is a *limit* rather than a bridge; where life is enclosed upon itself, sealed away from the monotony of the Sea.

The building in Aureli's island architecture is a singular image, within the universalizing frame of the Sea, that functions for the specific purposes of its own internal lives: the building attends to how the building is used, creating no universalizable principle.

> The islands are framed by this sea, yet their formal boundaries allow them to be understood as what frames and, to a certain extent, (re)defines the sea between the islands. Such an act of framing and redefinition consists not in the imposition of a general principle or of an overall norm, but in the strategic deployment of specific architectural forms that act as frames, and thus as a limit to urbanization.[23]

Lives lived on the islands—visible lives that are disallowed the freedom of invisible movement—have this benefit within their entrapment: they can bring dry land to the ampliative urbanization of the Sea. The visibility of the islands of racialized lives presents a challenge to the watery, homogenizing conquest of the Sea.

With his friend and fellow Black studies scholar Stefano Harney, American poet and philosopher Fred Moten began a tradition within Black studies called Black optimism, and its optimism lies precisely in recognizing and truly thinking about this advantage of entrapment—that within entrapment, languages and coded systems are made that are necessarily inaccessible to those who are free. Moten calls this 'the underprivilege of being-sentenced to the gift of constant escape'.[24] Having to constantly escape is no easy task. As White, carrying the global key of invisible movement, I do not know what it is. But I read Moten like a prayer book, like the gospel of escape, and his hymns are hammered into me. 'The burden of this paradoxically aleatory goal is our historicity, animating the reality of escape in and the possibility of escape from.'[25]

The island lives know a landed history that the Sea has no access to, and in that history its entire logic of global access collapses.

Going back to the beginning, Robert Lowell adds water to his parents' wet Sea-house by staying with his grandparents, doubling the parent dosage to the second level, from parents to parents' parents. What's he up to?

Lowell is a bourgeois poet who loves his pure American ancestry. He is the expansive product of the conquered land. The shape of Robert Lowell is what results when you spread yourself across a continent and call it your own. So all he has to hand is water; he is also the Sea. He wants to practise a poetics of rebellion, but he is miles from the endurance of the island. He is right in the middle of the growing water of the archipelago. So he brings water with him, double-dampening-down on his parents' martini Sunday. He arrives in sobriety, with water, resisting the hedonism of their own bourgeois performance. But he's wet, just like them.

The island is where the dry folk live out their hypervisible lives in the underprivilege of being sentenced to the gift of constant escape, and it is rebellion against a World of expanding Sea.

* * *

'HELP! MY OCEAN IS TURNING RED' captures the sentiment echoed so frequently by managers around the world. More and more people, whether managers of companies, heads of nonprofits, or leaders of government, find themselves up against an ocean of bloody competition and want to get out. Maybe your business is seeing its margins shrink. Maybe competition is getting more intense, driving commoditization of your offering and rising costs.[26]

This is the Blue Ocean Strategy of W. Chan Kim and Renée Mauborgne. The writers of *Blue Ocean Strategy* propose two kinds of ocean: one is red, one is blue. Quite simply, red is bad and blue is good. 'When we wrote Blue Ocean Strategy, we used the metaphor of red and blue oceans because red oceans seemed to capture the reality that organizations increasingly face, while blue oceans captured the endless possibility that organizations could create, as industry history has borne out since its inception.'[27]

The proposition is that, in order to successfully expand, companies have to create new oceans, multiplying the quantity of blue ocean contained in the World. Otherwise, the red ocean of no-profit appears.

The point, though, is not to get rid of red oceans. It is to learn how to conquer them, how to stay afloat inside them. In the red ocean, the limitation is that *there are limitations*. There are boundaries and borders and rigid coastlines, which create a blockage in profit-reproduction. While there will always be red-ocean-limitations to varying extents in the business World, the successful business-being must learn how to swim in order to establish more and greater blue oceans, which have no borders or limitations. In the blue ocean, expansion is infinite and necessary. The blue ocean always grows, and it makes its petty

Poseidons rich.

> Unfortunately, blue oceans are largely uncharted. The dominant focus of strategy work over the past thirty years has been on competition-based red ocean strategies. The result has been a fairly good understanding of how to compete skillfully in red waters...However, there is little practical guidance on how to create [blue oceans]. Without analytic frameworks to create blue oceans and principles to effectively manage risk, creating blue oceans has remained wishful thinking that is seen as too risky for managers to pursue as strategy. This book provides practical frameworks and analytics for the systematic pursuit and capture of blue oceans.[28]

What Kim and Mauborgne do not see is that they were born already in the blue ocean. The entire history that resulted in them and their global market is a history of making the blue ocean, and of capturing all other geographies and forms of life, and turning them into more blue ocean.

This book, Idi, provides impractical frameless works and psychoanalytics for the specific and singular use of islands

Kim and Mauborgne, and the millions of people who have swum in their big blue ocean, want to grow all the time. I don't know how they spend their evenings, their long years of bloating outwards. How do they wear clothes if they're always expanding in the blue ocean? I never understand the aesthetics of outwards movement. I'm too closed and quiet. I have nothing to say but just the amount of words sufficient for a book about fish and Bikini Girls. Nothing else.

Kim and Mauborgne get their work done 'not by focusing on the differences that separate customers but by building on the powerful commonalities across noncustomers to maximize the size of the blue ocean being created and new demand being

unlocked, hence minimizing *scale risk*.[29] Me, I'm like some kind
of fetish-fish for *scale risk*. All I want is tiny little spaces to stop
growing inside. I'm like a kinky lover of the miniscule, the island
life. All dried up, still a little red from the red ocean and all its
sexy boundaries, its hefty walls and STOP signs everywhere.
The red rubs off, onto me.

Everything written about the sea is written about connection,
about the links formed by the water in between populations.
Professor David Abulafia is in love with the way a World can be
formed out of the infinity of possibilities inside the expanding,
boundless sea.[30] Admiral James Stavridis is all about *sea power*, the
power of the water to carry people to each other, to ride into new
territory, marking the ideology of *territory* as the foundation of
World and its long roots of connection to everything.[31]

I like little boxes, Idi; tiny traps. I like the distant sound
of someone speaking who isn't here. I love the closedness of
bricks, the full life of concrete beneath my standing space, my
only space to stand.

* * *

I conducted a spontaneous survey of everyone who happened
to be in the same room as me on a particular day. I asked, 'Who
is the most famous bikini model in this here world?' And Genia
responded, 'Emily Ratajkowski.'

Emily Ratajkowski's father called her 'baby woman' because
she was 'a twelve-year-old with D cup breasts who still woke
up in the night and asked her mom to come and sleep in her
room'.[32]

What is 'woman' in this formulation? The formula set up is
that the qualifier *asking for mom* equals 'child' and the qualifier
(D cup) breasts equals 'adult'. These cannot exist together without
disjuncture: asking for mom requires no (D cup) breasts; having
(D cup) breasts requires not asking for mom.

It is quite striking that *breasts* are the bodily site of separation from the mother. The mother's breasts, in the nuclear structure, provide life to the baby; then, to stop being a baby, the child must firstly leave the mother's breasts and secondly create her own (D cup) breasts.

It's difficult to tell from Ratajkowski's analysis whether someone with C cup, B cup, or even A cup breasts would make a more coherent image of childhood, and therefore produce no disjuncture when asking for mom.

I don't have any breasts, Idi, and I suppose you don't either. When my mum hugs me she stands far away and leans forwards so that her breasts won't rub against my chest, avoiding the necessity of our relationship. My siblings think that this peculiar movement is because of her squeamishness around talking about or referencing sex with her children, but I think it's more than that.

If I feel my mother's breasts against my chest when I hug her, I am aware by haptic, pressed-up presence of the reason for this hug: I am alive because those breasts fed me when I was unable to feed myself. Those breasts are part of the motherness of the mother who mothered me, and that is a universal language that is not specific to us. Motherness is a breast-giving ceremony, and the child's rise is premised mythically and literally on the taking of the breast. In recognizing the presence of my mother's breasts, the language of our relationship is universal, growing forever like the Sea.

Hugging without breasts, though—or at least standing in a way that makes the breasts disappear—takes away the necessary historical reason for this hug. We are no longer embracing solely because of the requirements of life—she needs her children, I need my mother—but rather because we are two adult people who want to embrace, to show the proximity of our love. We create a specific and personal island language for our relationship, separated from the global practice of the mother-child relationship, on our own archipelagic mound resisting the Sea.

The liminal space of baby and woman that Ratajkowski lived in was not a domestic problem. Her parents allowed the emergence of Woman within the continuation of Baby, and the life of Baby not to be muffled by the inevitable rejection of Woman.

It was life outside the domestic space that caused problems.

As she entered the modelling industry at 15, an interesting shift of spaces occurred. The space of misogyny remained the same, emerging unknowingly out of relatives who warned Ratajkowski against showing her body and knowingly out of people who wanted to cause her harm. The caring space of domesticity, however, expanded to include the industry she worked in.

Her body was resident *as a body* inside these spaces of domesticity.

I see my naked body in the mirrors of all the places I've lived, privately dressing, going through my morning routine. I get ready for my day as one of my many roles in life—student, model, actress, friend, girlfriend, daughter, businesswoman. I look at my reflection and meet my own eyes. I hear the voices reminding me not to send the wrong message.

The domestic space is the containment of the naked body. Outside that space, the body is not a *naked body*. It is a body in the performance of certain social references: the student, the model, etc.

Her body *is a body* when it is in the comfortable (naked) space of home, which includes her working industry. Outside of that context, the body itself is slipped from that embodied meaning.

It's like this: architecture and the body create their meaning together, which then forms the urban structure of social referents. The 'small, ivy-covered, wood-floored home in Southern California' where Ratajkowski grew up is the *meaning* of the naked body for her; it is where her memories of her naked reflection—her private, personal, internal way of seeing herself—are built and held.

The meaning of my relationship to my mother is held in the fact of her breasts, in their use and their history. When she leans forwards and steps back as we embrace, she opens another kind of meaning in our relationship: a breastless form of knowing each other. She breaks the architectural significance of the mother and the son. We live anywhere, now, unbound from the space where she raised me.

Ratajkowski opens these otherwise architectures through the voices she hears when seeing the ghostly emergence of her naked body, in domestic spaces, away from the imaginary of anyone reading her articles, away from her home. 'And what is that message exactly?'

'Sexy' in contemporary culture means the labour factory of pornography, which is just hard work and the visuality of American capital accumulation, or it means a woman giving herself away to the Male Gaze, or it means unwavering belief in the plastic reproductions of Instagram's Photoshopped skin regime that gleams like medieval frescoes of Christ removed from any tangibility of the Jewish body.

Any medieval Christian who thought Christ was some unwashed Arab Jew was castigated, and anyone who believes Instagram celebrities are alive outside of Instagram receives a similar punishment.

None of that works. Ratajkowski wants to move away from moral punishments of those who fail to conform, and instead to explore the inwards space of domestic nudity, which Elizabeth Grosz sums up in unknowing collaboration with Ratajkowski, a single line of thought between model and philosopher:

The limits of possible spaces are the limits of possible modes of corporeality: the body's infinite pliability is a measure of the infinite plasticity of the spatiotemporal universe in which it is housed and through which bodies become real, are lived, and have effects.[33]

* * *

The bikini is the only piece of clothing that ever achieved such a distinguished aesthetic that it deems the body inside it worthy of itself. The bikini is not only a piece of clothing but a standard of body. A suit shows a certain Euro-American style of formality, a kimono shows Japanese status and style, a burka shows dedication to a religious code, but the bikini deems the body inside it *a bikini body*.

I search 'bikini' in an online bookshop and the results show something quite different to the playful, sexual meaning of the early bikini from the mid-twentieth century. The early bikini is all about the time away from work; it is the scene of a social performance conducted on beaches, on holidays, and even comes to signify the holiday itself. Once you're in a bikini—or looking at people in bikinis—then you're on holiday.

The bookshop results are all about work. *How to get a bikini body. How to get bikini body ready. How to prepare your bikini body.* The bikini might deem you worthy of it if you work hard enough, otherwise it will reject you. You might approach the bikini in spring, holding your towel up, but it turns to you in fury. It wraps itself tightly around the back of a chair and points a thin string at your embarrassed smile. 'You think *you* are worthy of *me*?! Haha!' and then it leaves, rejecting you again, another year in the pre-bikini misery that so quickly becomes the post-bikini infinity of middle age.

* * *

I unloaded a heavy wagon of hope when I started this, Idi. The load isn't any lighter now, but it's unburdened by directions.

* * *

In a talk in 2013, three-times-married father of one Howard Jacobson thinks of *his own* failure as the failure of *all literature*. When two publishers turned down his novel *The Finkler Question*, which later won the Booker Prize, he thought, 'Maybe this is no good. Maybe I've had it as a novelist. Maybe *we've* all had it as a novelist.' He figured that the novel as a form was on its way out. 'No one's reading seriously anymore, and when they are reading they're reading what I would consider *trash*.'[34] If Jacobson fails, *the whole world* fails. And that is what it means to be an...*artist*, in the celebrated and abstract World that defines itself against the embodied performances and domestic descriptions of *female artists*.

A year later, twice-divorced widower and father of four Will Self writes with absolute assurance, 'The novel is dead.' He stops writing momentarily to collect the £1,000,000 cheque from his latest novel, which—despite being formed of 800 pages of anachronistic Modernist packaging around one single joke—sells hundreds of thousands of copies. He pays the mortgage of his ample London home with the money he made from selling many novels, and then he continues writing about the total and absolute death of the novel.

What he abhors is 'the current dispensation, wherein those who reject the high arts feel not merely entitled to their opinion, but wholly justified in it. It goes further: the hallmark of our contemporary culture is an active resistance to difficulty in all its aesthetic manifestations, accompanied by a sense of grievance that conflates it with political elitism.'[35] And at that he storms off, wrapped in his prize money that protects him from the throes of his lowly life, as son of Professor Peter Self, grandson of Sir Henry Self.

There is writing on the wall, and Self is profiting from it. But the writing also seems to speak to others, unable to fully offer him the entirety of its fame and money. So he gets angry. He goes for long walks, crushing London under his long and famous body.

Joyce Carol Oates, who once wrote something that someone liked and that person happened to be in charge of putting together school curricula, complains about books she doesn't like on Twitter. The poet and novelist A. K. Blakemore responded to Oates, and I can't respond any better, so I won't bother. Oates remains, I suppose, angry about books that are not by her.

Property-investor who dreams of becoming a famous buy-to-rent landlord Lionel Shriver wishes that everyone would write about someone they are not, specifically for the purpose of offensive literature. Literature, if anything, needs to be *more offensive*, because in Shriver's protected millionaire world of fame and global recognition, she just doesn't see enough suffering, so maybe we need more of it in books. 'I don't write novels with a prissy little pen in my hand.'[36] No sir; she has the latest MacBook, and she's not afraid to use it. She'll write a novel not only *about* you but *as* you if you dare question rich White people's ability to be universal, to exist as global reason. Why not put a hand on someone's knee without them asking? Why not pretend to need a wheelchair in your next epic? Fuck it.

A father of two who was married to Jeanne Gould for over 60 years, Harold Bloom was deeply unhappy about the state of the novel, which was not so much too dead, but rather alive in the wrong way. 'We are now in an era of so-called "cultural criticism", which devalues all imaginative literature, and which particularly demotes and debases Shakespeare.'[37]

I once went out with Shakespeare on a date, but he hadn't changed his tights in so long that they had grown into his leg hair. I left, horny, before the Enlightenment, and haven't read him since.

What do you do, Idi, when you are in love with literature, with all the sounds of art, and its raging life, but everyone who looks like you is saying it's all dead?

I suppose you know already that I don't really ask to find an answer.

But I think, somehow, that reading, studying, and loving lots of writers who are called *female artists*, *Black artists*, or even *Black female artists* can teach us all we need to know to make us love the life of writing.

I would invite the *artists* who are stuck on the hatred of their own disappearance, the sudden realization that the World is not solely here for them, but they don't seem to be listening. Maybe we shouldn't have soundproofed the Institute.

* * *

Idi, I want to introduce you to Hunter Ledbetter. He refers to the kinds of people who go fishing and get caught inside the frame as 'fishing girls'. Patrik Alac, uncannily, refers to them by the archetype 'the girl in the bikini'.

The girl in the bikini in this way adopts a measured way of walking, a style in which she can proceed provocatively along the beach, and make the best of all her bodily qualities. She uses certain provocative gestures she has seen—but not so that anyone could accuse her of being at all indecent. Her arms may be above her head, exposing her armpits; she may stride with her hips, like a mannequin on the catwalk; she may seem playful, lost in her thoughts, twisting the strap of her bikini around her little finger (suggesting quite clearly a character stronger than her body language—enough to twist a man she fancies around her little finger too).[38]

After writing his book about the bikini, Patrik Alac falls off his chair and cries, incomparably distraught that no woman in a bikini ever fancied Patrik Alac enough to twist him around her bikini fingers.

It's quite incredible how wrong Patrik Alac can be about the meaning of a pose. For Alac, everything is a performance for men. The observer is Universal, he is the expanding Sea, and he is called Patrik Alac. He observes with a hand in his pocket, hiding his electric hard-on.

What he is remarkably unable to see is the private space behind the performance of the Fishing Girl. There is so much going on in the folds of polyester bands, behind the surface of the body's cartographic skin, in excess of the pointing map directions. But Alac is blind to all of it, his vision distorted by the signs that point towards almost naked boobs.

* * *

Pier Vittorio Aureli tries to think the city against the Sea of urbanization in various ways. He is interested in the island that resists becoming the Sea. In the archipelago, the Sea strokes the edges of islands constantly, gradually shifting stones and sand until everything is the Sea, but some islands resist. They remain islandy. These are the sites of Aureli's architectural fantasy, the places he wants to live his ascetic life on.

In one book, he calls this *the possibility of absolute architecture*, an architecture so absolute that it only refers to itself: an island that speaks to itself as island, in the language of an island, against the Sea that homogenizes its islandness.[39]

In a slightly earlier essay, he calls it *Stop City*, a form of urban space that seals itself off from the endless lines of connection in the totalizing map of urbanization.

The main thesis of *Stop City* stems from the observation that today the relationship between those who live and work in the city and the city itself recalls the relationship that workers once had with the factory during the era of industrial expansion. If the factory was dominated by the spatially and temporally choreographed rhythm of the assembly line, today's cities are dominated by the pervasive informality of social relationships, which subsume every aspect of human communication and cognition as a factor of production. In other words, the contemporary city, in spite of its increasing complexities, contradictions, and informalities, has been reduced to the contemporary factory, and its inhabitants have (potentially) become the new working class.[40]

The city of the Sea, City Everywhere, is the endless labour of communication. To live there is to never stop conducting the unpaid work of unreeling rhizomes. You have to speak and grow in order to push into the blue ocean, against the heavy limitations of the red ocean, or what I—with Aureli—prefer to call islands.

The Sea is where men go fishing, Idi, and where Bikini Girls go, too. They love the blue ocean, its infinity. It's all they talk about. Oh, and also bikinis.

* * *

I was speaking to an actor and she told me that there are three elements that make her as an actor, a triangle of subjectivities that form Her: the *actor*, the *acted character*, and the *private person*. She was particularly interested in how the English actor Emma Watson deals with these three subjectivities, allowing each to emerge with its own attitude and seriousness.

The speaking body of Emma Watson takes each of her three positions seriously, not letting any ridicule another. As she says in an interview,

It's about finding that line between being spontaneous and open to direction, but also trying to explain to photographers that the 'me' is often taken out of context because it has all of this other stuff attached to it. The fact that I was a child star is difficult for most people to understand, and it can be really conflicting for me. Photographers want to reinvent you, to take you somewhere else, to show you in a completely different way. They look at your previous work, and try to figure out what they can do to show a new side of you.[41]

Photographers find the coordinates of the 'child star' and expand them to the size of the frame. They pre-emptively Photoshop the child to an adult stature, and resist touching the frame of their own belief: the tiny lens through which they see Emma Watson/Hermione Granger.

Watson's Granger fits into a small pocket, though, or a case on the windowsill. Another Watson is held in a private space within that fantasy of the child: the world of Granger, which ultimately is the world that afforded Watson her enormous fame and wealth, was a world of enacted fantasy, a reality of fantasy piles of money and photographers and red carpets, and that is where the space of privacy is kept.

The private Watson is not disconnected or external to the lived *Harry Potter* fantasy Watson. Crucially, they share a purse and a public image.

Watson wants to keep that private space internal to the fantasy quite separate. However, she also reveals how much it is created and shaped by the people who *direct* her, who photograph her and write her lines and organize her celebrity diary. 'Artists have given me a lot of freedom—have been able to imagine me in other ways,' she says, tuned to this celebrity movement as a kind of *freedom*, but freedom of course within the restrictions of being observed. It is the freedom to be what someone told her to be.

Freedom anyway is not the ability to live without taking suggestions from anyone else; that's libertarianism. For Watson, freedom is the ability to believe in the privacy of that space within the conflation of her selves as actor and as character: where Emma Watson the Actor and Emma Watson as Hermione Granger the Character merge, a tiny space opens, in those intricate seams, and that space is what freedom means for Watson.

The space, possibly, has nothing inside it and would open nothing up for another person. But that makes no difference at all. This is not a material investment in property; it is not the pursuit of a house or another human form. (I'm sure Watson has more than enough houses for many lifetimes.) This is a pursuit of belief. The point is to *believe* that more possibilities can be opened through the space between the actor who occupies most of her time and the character who allowed the actor to give her time to acting. 'But I know that if I live in that fear, then my life as an artist, as a human being, really, is over. Ultimately, it will silence me, and it will silence what is in me—which I have yet to explore and uncover.'

There's a side of this that's a standard prompt of liberal feminism: the woman has to believe in herself, stop all this 'intellectualizing' and 'self-analyzing' (as Watson decrees) and 'be in your body' which is difficult but your body is beautiful, etc. As much as that might mean, this is not the place for liberal feminism and I am obviously not the person to write the manifestoes for it. This is the Institute of Maritime Images, Etc., and we are here to have conversations with Hunters and Bikini Girls.

So there's another side of what she's saying, or many other sides. I can't see all the sides, of course, because *look at me!* Goddamn! But I can see one other side.

Watson says that the audience needs to be able to suspend their disbelief while watching an actor play a character, which is often cut in her case by the emergence of Hermione Granger within Emma Watson. But really she knows that's not what's going on. True—when an amazing actor plays a brilliant character, you totally forget the fiction. But more important than that is that the *actor herself* can suspend her disbelief in any separation between actor, character, and private person.

The actor usually is inseparable from characters. Does Watson go to school? Yes. Does she fall in love and have close friends and battle daemons? Of course. Can she fly? Probably—I don't know, I've never met her. Hermione Granger and Emma Watson are not different.

But then the private person assumes her position as actor, and the actor must be separable from the character. Suddenly it is impossible for the actor to believe that she could ever be the character, because then she wouldn't be an actor. She can only become the character on the condition that she is no longer an actor.

I suppose that has happened to actors before—sliding into the otherwise reality of the character, finding themselves unable to emerge into belief in themselves as actors rather than characters.

But it doesn't happen to Watson. While the audience is suspending their disbelief in the possibility of a *unity* between actor and character (the audience says: indeed, now *actor and character can be one single thing!*), the actor Watson is suspending her disbelief in the possibility of a *separation* between actor and character (she says to herself: indeed, now *I must be an actor because I am playing a character*, and therefore actor and character *are necessarily not the same!*). While the audience realizes her as character, she realizes herself as actor.

Her belief in that private space of personal, bodily being between actor and character is the space that audiences can never know. We can access so much of Watson's life—I was able to find out all sorts of things about her daily practice, her beliefs, her desires, just from a few hours researching this little section at our watery Institution, Idi. But what we cannot access — what I and no audience will ever know — is her own *belief* in that private space, that plot of land in which we are not allowed to believe because if we did then we'd never be able to watch her films, and then she'd stop getting paid and hired and then she'd stop being an actor. If we accessed that belief in the private space, we would kill the tripartite Watson.

Watson says that her life is lived under a 'microscope', a *'different* microscope, a certain level of scrutiny'. The method of the microscope is quite a peculiar way of seeing. Using a *telescope*, we define our own subjectivity as central against our definition of the thing we are looking at as *far away*, since we are looking at it through a telescope. A telescope, really, is a machine for defining certain things as peripheral, so that we can define the viewer (ourselves) as central.

The microscope, though, has quite a different purpose. It seeks to define its object as *internal*. We look at things through microscopes that are so small they constitute us. We look at the diseases inside us and the subvisible matter that makes the things we see.

Being seen through a microscope is to be defined as the internal matter of the body that does the looking. The audience looks at Watson through a microscope and by that process we understand Watson as *inside us*, as *creating us* with her atomic performances.

Her body is taken away from her by the way we look at her. But her body re-emerges in a private space in which we necessarily can never believe, otherwise our way of seeing would be ruined.

Emma Watson is a machine for a certain kind of social seeing, Idi. I just wanted you to know that, since it's been on my mind in this long winter, cement clouds building paradisiac chariot parking above me, on the long wave of grey. I just want you to know that with me, Idi.

* * *

Idan Hayosh is also split into three. He divides the coordinates of his subjectivity according to a triangle of intersecting roles.

There is Idan (a.k.a. Idi to his friends), the private person, the man from Israel going to the supermarket and paying his rent in Essen, Germany; Idan Hayosh, the artist, the silent producer of loud artworks; and Idi, the character in the stories on Idan's Instagram account, @idi_thrice_removed.

Idan the private person, who is called Idi to his friends, wants me to know that the character Idi and all his stories on Instagram are *not* the same as his other work. He writes emails to me in different colours and typewriter fonts:

> i gotta write you about the context of the instagram posts, and its relation to my day job [as an artist]. it's of importance for now that u understand that for me, those posts are 100% hobby i do in my pastime.

For a moment it looks like Idan the Man doesn't take Idi the Character seriously, but that's just a ruse. It's a confusion of which angle of the triangle connects to the character Idi. If I take the emails as coming from the artist Idan Hayosh then he is dismissing a part of his creation; he is creating balances and universal equivalents of value between one artwork and another, which would undermine a continuous seriousness.

But these emails are not from Idan Hayosh the Artist. They are from Idan the Man, the private person, the Jew in Germany. The character Idi comes out of the man Idan without direct mediation from the artist Idan Hayosh.

It's hard to tell the two apart. They are both resistant to over-speaking.

In 2013, the first people to interview him were immediately caught in this confusion, looking between the angles of the triangle for signs as to who is saying what, and finding nothing.

Idan Hayosh normally doesn't give interviews. Ours is his first, says the serious-minded 34-year-old. He never talks about his work, has never seen the point. He wants his works to speak for themselves. And they do. The installations with which Hayosh made a name for himself do not need to be explained or put in a context; no art-historical references are required. They're simply there. They cannot be overlooked, are unmistakable. You can't escape them. And you'll remember them for the rest of your life.[42]

The other option is to write a whole book about him and his artworks and their involvement with fish and women in bikinis. Whichever you prefer, *baby*.

* * *

Idi, I drop all this pain at your door. I don't want it back. And I'm sorry for leaving it with you. Chuck it in the ocean, if you want. For now, at least. Even though it'll soon wash back over you. And me.

* * *

The maps etched into and as the cartography of the body can be changed by Emma Watson and Emily Ratajkowski. They can manipulate the meaning of the lines in their skin, the historical constitution of the body's social semantics.

Ratajkowski seals her meaning inside a personal referent of *home*, which becomes a place where her nudity is allowed to reflect itself in reflecting surfaces: mirrors, family, spouse, children, memories. For Watson, there is a little space that opens up only to her between the embracing forms of Character and Actor. In the split of that suspension, a gap opens, and that gap is a private space in which only Watson can believe, and Watson can only be Watson while she believes in that space and its privacy.

Bodies are given very different coordinates of meaning, though. American cultural theorist Sianne Ngai writes about the ways in which the history of racial capitalism has managed the emotional coding of bodies. Since the Enlightenment in Europe, 'rationality' has been the engine of liberal pursuits of homogeneous globalization, attempting to formulate a single idea of human scale: at the top, the most rational (i.e. the least emotional)—White, European, able-bodied, married and heterosexual man, with property; at the bottom, the least rational (i.e. the most emotional)—Black, non-European, disabled, queer or trans woman, without property.

Since the early twentieth-century form of factory-line production called Fordism, as Ngai writes, the meaning of the human has emerged in tandem with the requirements of capitalist production. Taking Immanuel Kant's idea of the ideally rational, disinterested, and objective man to its extremity, the organization of the factory-line requires humans to perform regimented and repetitive tasks without the superfluity of feeling. Being overly moved or agitated becomes a marker of barbarism, through which the agitated or moved body is marked in the logics of race, gender, sexuality, and ability.

Ngai calls this form of being moved 'animatedness', and explains how it functions 'as a marker of racial or ethnic otherness'.

[T]he cultural representation of the African-American... most visibly harnesses the affective qualities of liveliness, effusiveness, spontaneity, and zeal to a disturbing racial epistemology, and makes these variants of 'animatedness' function as bodily (hence self-evident) signs of the raced subject's naturalness or authenticity.[43]

The Black person in the USA is coded with a form of over-emotion, with animatedness, which is situated *in the body*, creating a corporeal national code as nature: the African body is *naturally* animated, and therefore too irrational to function within the production processes of capitalism. This has been used historically to justify and maintain plantation slavery, the contemporary prison industry, and infinite instances of quotidian violence.

In the liberal imaginary, race is generally understood as something natural. *Blacks are good at running*, says someone. My auntie, or yours. There is some natural categorization of forms of life. Where racism is recognized within this nature, it is recognized as a mechanism of *removal*. Women, *female artists*, Black and Brown and Indigenous and Asian people, are removed from the central privilege of society's space. But removal, really, makes a person invisible. Being removed is what Emma Watson does in the space of her belief, that tiny nodal point between the already-scripted character and the constantly-observed actor. She turns herself invisible.

What theorists—or *female artists*, maybe I should say, since we are, after all, at the Institution of Maritime Images, Etc.—like Ngai, Grosz, Tadiar, Brown, Hong, Philip, and King are saying is that, firstly, race isn't *natural*. That's not the temporal order. Rather, *nature is racial*. It's not that there was an objective and neutral thing called nature, and it made a thing called race, giving some bodies darkness because they spent generations around the equator and other bodies lightness because they spent ages outside the tropics. Instead, a system of social referents called *race* was created and then justified by the invention of a thing called *nature*, which makes propositions non-negotiable. Why are Black people enslaved, why imprisoned, why murdered without blame? Nature. It's just nature, now. American nature is racist genocide. That's a reason in itself.

Secondly, racialization isn't the process of becoming invisible. It's the process of becoming *hyper*visible. Invisibility is a privilege. Those who can transcend the global logic of borders and checks and stops, those who can sweep in with the rising tide of the growing Sea. That's magic. Other people are always spotted in the line. They're always observed, seen, registered, and checked.

It's a long story, Idi, but basically in January 2011 I got caught up in the Arab Spring in Tunisia. At some point, I had to leave Tunis, so I ran to a government building, which was surrounded by armed guards. I have no diplomatic connections, no social value through my job, and know no one in high Tunisian society. But the guards let me through without question, the universal ticket of my Whiteness parting seas. Inside the armed ring, there were taxis, which were now impossible to get anywhere else in the capital.

The airport had been seized by the army and closed. Twenty kilometres away in the ancient city of Carthage, the port was the only way out.

The taxi driver told me to hide under the front seats; I dropped down from the back and stuffed myself in. We drove in silence, me in darkness, for half an hour.

The port was packed with people. The scene was unbelievable—people everywhere, screaming, arguing with port staff who had all but given up their jobs by this point, people dragging their entire lives behind them.

Many hours later, the doors of a ferry opened. There was no way of checking tickets or assigning spaces within the boat. Everyone ran towards it. I was smoking a cigarette when it happened so I got off to a delayed start, stuck behind a gradually slowing crowd, packed all the way from the deck to the port waiting room. An old man was limping in front of me and I carried his bag. He gave me a full pack of cigarettes.

Finally, I got into the boat. All the cabins were closed off and every surface was covered with people. The floor was made of thousands of bodies now, people who had been awake and electrified with stinging anxiety for hours and hours, on top of the anxiety of war. I put down my bag on a little patch beside the closed bar and went outside to smoke and get some fresh air, as everyone else was smoking inside.

When I came back, someone was asleep on my bag. I sat on the bar counter and dozed, chatting to a young man, about the same age as me, in a mix of languages we just about spoke. When the man on my bag awoke, he got to his feet with difficulty, yawned, patted me on the back and held open a pack of cigarettes.

At the port in Palermo we all waited in a queue that seemed endless. Italian guards checked out the crowd. There must have been thousands of people, mostly Tunisian men.

A guard spotted me. I saw him double-take and frown. He approached me. I showed him my British passport and he escorted me out of the crowd, right to the front, without even touching me—the full VIP treatment of Whiteness, separated from the Arab crowd. I was allowed to walk through the gates of the port, into Sicily and the winter sunshine. My Whiteness and its attendant guarantee of citizenship opened the arch of Europe for me.

It's astounding how successful the logic of race has become over 6 centuries. It manages to deem certain populations as *vulnerable* because of their surplus of emotion, their animatedness, and that vulnerability is also *dangerous*—the fact that they are irrational makes them capable of *anything*.

Look, the thing is, when you say *Blacks can run quickly* and you support the Jamaican Olympic team, Idi, you're also saying *Slaves can escape the plantation quickly*. We cannot be so dismissive of the history and historiography that got us here, to this stage in the global genocide of the Sea, that we find that unbelievable. And Trinidadian-Canadian writer Dionne Brand certainly does not find it unbelievable. 'The Black body,' as she writes, 'is a kind of "naturalized" body in the popular culture. Appreciated in athletes, musicians, singers; absent in the public discourse as associated with the scientific—the scientific being the remaining range of activity, activity having formal authority. She magnificently adds, 'In Western culture, the natural is always captive to science.'[44]

American cultural theorist Stephen Pokornowski explains the complexity of this historical operation of race.

> [It is a] double-bind—the vulnerable is at once that which wounds and that which is susceptible to being wounded… To put it plainly: those who are most vulnerable are also perceived…as the most dangerous…Thus, the limits of humanity (and perhaps innocence) are constantly being shifted by complex assemblages of political relations (race, racialization, sex, sexuality, ability) around the vulnerability of life.[45]

Race here is a logic that *creates* the codes of *nature*, ordering bodies along a scale of naturalness that allows some privileged forms of life (Whiteness, masculinity) to be further from nature, and so further from race, and so more self-protected, and so less dangerous, while making other forms of life (Blackness, the *female artist*) more vulnerable, and thus more dangerous. As Ngai says, this 'reinforc[es] the notion of race as a truth located, quite naturally, in the always obvious, highly visible body'.[46]

American queer and race theorist Jasbir K. Puar adds to this a discussion of the *disabling* of queer, trans, and racialized bodies. The process of becoming racialized, queered, and trans is a process of being rendered into a shape that cannot fit the prescriptions of racist rationality. That twisted shape, however, traps the body even deeper in the violent mechanisms of appropriation. The racialized queer/trans body is not *removed* from the system that enforces hierarchical homogeneity; it is stuck even deeper inside it. 'The debilitating and abjecting [of bodies] are cosubstancing processes.'[47] To racialize a body as abject, it must also be debilitated from the possibility of removing itself from the mechanism of racialization.

Each category is placed on a complex trajectory of relation to the rational summit. Each category of the body has to connect somehow to the apex of capital's invisible body-regime in order for it to be productive for the cultural, social, and exchange value of the economy.

Puar traces these networks through the Whitening of queer activism, allowing certain queer bodies into the privileged invisibility of Whiteness, and through the pharmacological industry that profits from the medical reassignment of gender through hormonal treatments, subsuming the trans body in the productivity of pharma capital.

The question is how transsexual and disabled bodies are assigned social meaning. In both the discourses of transsexuality and disability, 'normativization' is the objective.[48]

Transsexuality is *treated* with prosthetics, medication, hormonal enhancement, and even behavioural manipulation in order to turn the body from a nonconforming mode to a paradigm of ableist conformance. The trans body is pharmacologically presented as a body on its way to becoming non-disabled. So, while *transitioning* is presented as a process of becoming sexually non-normative, it simultaneously relocates the body within the code of ability as *no longer disabled*. It has been redeemed by corrective medicine. 'Thus, trans relation to disability is not simply one of phobic avoidance of stigma; it is also about trans bodies being recruited, in tandem with many other bodies, for a more generalized transformation of capacitated bodies into viable neoliberal subjects.'[49]

Puar sees disability in the global capitalist economy as a raw material that is used by nonconforming bodies to code themselves as successfully becoming the Sea—becoming conformant in the visuality of the economy—through their movement away from and out of disability. 'Seen through this mechanism of resource extraction, disability is the disavowed materiality of a trans embodiment that abstracts and thus effaces this materiality from its self-production.'[50] Trans bodies disavow their relation to disability in order to enter the valuable framework of transsexuality given by the fetishizing value-form of a liberal way of seeing.

There are coordinates in the violence of the Sea that allow movement outwards, the invisible privilege of being able to expand with water. There are other coordinates in the Sea that disallow any kind of shift. Whiteness is such a powerful coordinate in the logics of the Sea that it allows the movement of all other forms, to varying extents. While sexuality, gender, ability, nationality, religion, and ethnicity have the power to hinder movement, when they are aligned with Whiteness they can move anyway. Masculinity is another strong coordinate. Lacking both coordinates makes all other coordinates more hindering to movement in the Sea.

The body is divided into pieces, into the atomic matter of coordinating codes, regulating the meaning of life in the Sea. This is what Puar calls the 'bodies with new organs' in her essay's title. The new organs are the range of complex coordinates that bodies are split into for the purposes of widely applicable value-reproduction: disability is accumulated and circulated in a different way to transsexuality, and they are both configured on a different line to race and gender, although they cross each other often.

The heaviness of lines moving over the skin of bodies, Idi— it's so unbearable to think of. The difficulty of the language written into our existences.

Watson and Ratajkowski can move through the abstract referents of *(self-)belief* because they are also within the coordinating structure of Whiteness, and English Britishness and US Americanness respectively. The coordinates of feminized gendering are slightly eased by the cohering value of their Whiteness. On top of that, they're rich and famous, so anyway they do whatever the fuck they want.

* * *

One thing that is important, Idi, is that the language we have at our use to talk about these things is insufficient to really talk about these things. Like Spanish writer and philosopher Paul Preciado says, 'trans' is some bullshit word that tries to make it sound like the people who refuse gender are the ones in *transition*, the ones who are unstable and unable to conform to the requirements of binary gendering. But *trans* should be the word for anyone who still believes in the bullshit nonsense of binary gender.[51] Obviously, all of humanity cannot be categorized into only two genders. The binary system is far too simplistic and expansive; it attempts to subsume everything into one of only two types. How can my manness link me inextricably to you, Idi, and to Jesus of Nazareth and Fred Moten of Las Vegas? What could possibly link us through the nexus of things called manness, masculinity, or the...*artist*?

Preciado, having refused the stupidity of binary gender and become not-this-or-that, is the non-trans one among us, in these paragraphs. We're trans, Idi, because we're still in the transitional phase of calling ourselves 'men' before we come to the better realization that we are obviously not.

* * *

The photographer of many of these fishy women, whom he calls 'Fishing Girls', is a retired marine from the US Army called Hunter Ledbetter. He works in Florida's Key West.

Is Hunter chasing fish, the kill, or the mythical 'women' who have achieved the status of bikini body? There is one single photograph of Hunter himself holding a dead fish on his Instagram account. The fish is certainly part of his pursuit. But far more common than dead fish, women in bikinis are featured, all preceded in the description by the intro 'your girl' and then her Instagram account name. 'Here in Key West with your girl @FishingGirl', for example.

His name, remember, is Hunter.

* * *

Some bodies begin with the impossibility of moving subjectivity. Some bodies are held in place, by definition. This occurs over centuries through a political and economic decision—summarized as capitalism—to merge the meaning of *land* and *bodies*. Bodies that are *on the land* are bodies that are not universal, not freely wafting over global currents of capital.

Within this movement, a global narrative has to be established that marks a *temporal* frame for conquest: the conquerors are looking towards the *Future*, where endless profit is, and the conquered are the *Past*, getting in the way of progress.

This idea of global progressive time remains profoundly influential in the society we live in, Idi, in this mature stage of global capitalism. Politicians still happily describe the *civilizing mission* of the West, the goal of turning the rest of the World into our peripheral proxies. People talk despairingly of how those far-away Muslims treat women, and how they should be subsumed into the perfect liberal practices of Western nations, conveniently forgetting the power of our own misogynist regime that strictly divides social function and worth by gender assignment. Some women are allowed to be abused, raped, and murdered in order for the worth of bourgeois White women to be affirmed.

Within the global movement of capitalist time, there is also a sexualized difference marked in feminized bodies. The *lascivious* woman is *uncivilized*, making her dispensable. Her reproductivity only functions for appropriation, for being *used*, not for the civilized feminized labour of reproducing labourers. 'White men, the endowed rulers of this racist and sexist heteropatriarchal system,' American race and sex theorist Mireille Miller-Young writes, 'justified their sexual coercion of black women by arguing that not only did black women's lascivious ontology and "relaxed morals" make them willing participants, but the degraded and "casual" nature of sex with them protected white female chastity.'[52]

In the fifteenth century, Africa is turned into appropriable land. Its people can be stolen as bodies for the reproduction of value, in order that fully Human (White) people did not have to engage in the arduous and deadly toil of plantation production, the low labour of maritime piracy, and servitude. Accordingly, the African *body* is turned into an attendant commodity of African *land*. Blackness as Slave is a narrative enforced globally, which evidently survives today, given the legal exemption the police have while murdering Black people.

As Miller-Young elaborates, it's a circular logic that stamps certain forms of life with a label and then justifies gratuitous violence because of the label; because of the maps written into the body, the cartographic token of violation. Throughout the centuries-long regime of Euro-Americans enslaving Africans, Black feminized bodies were rapeable commodities. This systemic rape was justified by a proposed *natural* difference in racialized bodies: White women reproduce according to the Christian logic of patriarchal family hierarchy, while Black women are lascivious and incapable of achieving the civility of misogyny. 'This unfeeling, vulgar kind of sex,' Miller-Young writes, 'rubs up against expectations of personal morality and rational social values rooted in traditional, bourgeois views of sex for the reproduction of proper families and citizens.'[53]

British race and geological theorist Kathryn Yusoff investigates the processes of land and bodies in their emergent forms as violated life in capitalism: '[a]s land is made into tabula rasa for European inscription of its militant maps, so too do Indigenes and Africans become rendered as a writ or ledger of flesh scribed in colonial grammars'.[54] Colonial grammars are the cartographic language of modern capitalism, its coordinates of conquest, its outwards movement into islands, as the Sea, that writes the meanings of value all over bodies. The land as heterogeneous *earth* is subsumed into singular World, as the bodies of humans are turned into the racialized lack of being Human. In the land is written the people's distance from being White Men, and that land is the body — its race, its gender, its normativity.

There are circles of meaning surrounding human life and land. Every sight registers multiple social meanings and a value estimate is given to every scene. The women on the yachts, Idi, are almost all White. There are only four non-White women on Idan's Instagram account, at the Institute of Maritime Images, Etc. Two are light-skinned Black women (*February 15, 2021*, and (maybe) *August 19, 2020*), another (*July 22, 2019*) is clothed and on land, removing her from the semantics of the Sea, and the other (*October 20, 2018*), significantly, is neither fishing nor on a boat: she is at a beach where a whale has incidentally died, and she is separated from it by a line of tape that cordons off the corpse.

Something about the coordinates of race make hunting on the Sea a White activity of conquest.

Conquest requires the logic of expansion. To move out, into and as the Sea — conquering life and reformulating it as life subjected to Human power—requires a bodily cartography that means outwards movement. To be on a yacht with a rod, you need your body to refer to a history of imperial expansion and domination, otherwise the sense is lost. To be a hunter on a boat, to be invisible enough to float universally and kill without question, you need to have a kind of meaning called White, which means Human in the World. Like Tiffany Lethabo King says:

> Black bodies are, in fact, the spatial coordinates that the human can manipulate and inhabit. Early geographical imaginaries posited 'space as outside of human existence.' Black bodies, one with nature, take on the coordinates of space within Western thought. Black bodies mark the outsides of humanness.[55]

Black bodies are *beyond* the Human form of the Sea. Black bodies are on islands, resisting the centuries of their enslavement, enduring the anti-Black genocide of modernity, and making a new grammar of islandness, a radical language specific to the archipelago.

And you can't hunt while taking photos of women in bikinis on islands, Idi, because the yacht is the necessary land of this scene; a land that signifies global domination, a plastic land that means the Sea.

There is something about Blackness, *past* and *beyond* the Human, that cannot be captured in contemporary culture's visual frameworks. For Tiffany King and Fred Moten, this is Blackness's fugitivity, its life as fugitive, fleeing into the possibility of a better future, of a rethought time to come, as islands in the archipelago.

* * *

American writer and actor Lena Waithe says that she wants to make art that 'humanizes Black people', because when the 'gunman' notices a Black person's *humanity*—such as by the Black person in the sightlines of the gun saying that her mother is sick in hospital, or that she has a child—he is less likely to shoot. Immediately afterwards, Waithe says that her 2019 film *Queen & Slim* is not an 'anti-cop movie'.[56]

In *Queen & Slim*, two young Black people meet on a Tinder date in an Ohio restaurant. Slim (Daniel Kaluuya) offers Queen (Jodie Turner-Smith) a ride home. As Slim reaches for his phone, the car swerves slightly, and they are pulled over by the police. The White police officer is enraged with signature racist wrath and draws his gun. As Queen demands to be given a reason for this violence, the policeman shoots her in the leg. Slim tackles the officer. There is a fight. Slim takes the police gun and shoots the policeman dead. The rest of the film is their attempt to escape to Cuba, driving all the way down to Florida to find a plane.

In the film, Black characters speak to each other with no visual signs of speech. At a New Orleans bar, while dancing with closed mouths, Slim looks up at Queen. 'What do *you* want?' he asks. 'I want a guy to show me myself...I want him to show me scars I never knew I had. But I don't want him to make them go away. I want him to hold my hand while I nurse them myself. And I want him to cherish the bruises they leave behind,' she responds, all with closed lips.[57]

A while later, they are walking by the port with the son of a mechanic who is fixing their car. They sit beside the water. Without moving their mouths, the mechanic's son says that it will be OK even if they do not make it, if they do not manage to escape the murderous will of the police. 'How so?' asks Queen. 'Because then you'll be immortal.' 'I like that,' says Slim. 'I'd rather live,' Queen adds. 'I want to be immortal too,' says the son.

In a subsequent scene, the young mechanic's son will shoot a police officer in the head.

'I just want people to know I was here,' says the son. 'As long as your family knows you were here, that's all that matters,' Queen says, repeating Slim's earlier statement about his desire to cut the fugitive escape and return to his family.

The family here seems to be a specifically Black linguistic entity. *Knowing you are here* emerges through this subtle form of speech that cannot be registered by the visual frameworks of the camera. There is an autochthonous kind of Black American language that folds the communication between Black people — as a family, as a network with a particular form of historical meaning — into a sonic undercurrent, beyond the camera and the visuality of the audience.

While it has been criticized for repeating the fatal danger of being Black in America, affirming the status as fugitive and murder-object of the law that precedes the lives of all Black Americans, what the film manages to portray is the law's lack of reasoning for its murderous racism. The police are not given time in the film's narrative to explain themselves. In our World, police explanations fill the newspapers, stuff the mouths of politicians with repeatable and eternal motifs of Black-blaming, and allow the White population to dismiss this emergence of an ongoing genocide as a singular and accidental event.

In so many movies about racist violence and the inherent genocidal function of the state, time is offered on screen for the police, the courts, the law, and the politicians to explain themselves, to render the narrative into the normative mould of their established procedures.

Queen & Slim refuses the ceremony of presenting this violence as a *debate*. Genocide is not a debate. There is no conversation to be had about centuries of enslavement and systematic murder and entrapment. There is no dialectic in process between the forces of the state's White supremacy and the resistance of the enduring island of Blackness. There is, instead, conquest. Conquest is a logic that spreads itself out everywhere, collapsing the lives of everything beneath it. The state is a spatial logic that establishes itself—like architecture on the land—over and *as* the World. Nothing can be spoken when it is spoken in the logic of the racist state.

In a liberal argument—or a *political* argument, that engages with the visual domain of life that is politics—the inevitable condition of *Queen & Slim*'s protagonists as murdered Black flesh is difficult to swallow. Why can something *good, positive, uplifting* and Black not be culturally created? In this view, Black *life* and Black *lives* are the same thing; those who are alive and how they live are what define the ontological condition that is Blackness.

However, for two groups of radical Black scholars— Afropessimists, and Black optimists—there is a great difference between *life* and *lives*.

For Afropessimist Professor of African American Studies Jared Sexton, the condition of Black lives in American modernity is captivity, and captivity is outside of the normative time of America; there is a 'slow time of captivity, the dilated time of the event horizon, the eternal time of the unconscious'.[58] That slow and long captivity produces a jarring form of questioning in Black lives. As the White supremacist ideology that is 'America' relies on the proposition of Black anti-subjectivity, in which Blacks are anti-life, Black lives present an impossible form of questioning: 'What is the nature of a form of being that presents a problem for the thought of being itself? More precisely, what is the nature of a human being whose human being is put into question radically and by definition, a human being whose being human raises the question of being human at all?'[59]

This political, or juridical, (anti-)position is what Fred Moten calls 'the lived experience' of Blackness, which is defined against the 'fact' or the 'case' of Blackness. Moten asks:

how the troubled, illicit commerce between fact and lived experience is bound up with that between blackness and the black, a difference that is often concealed, one that plays itself out not by way of the question of accuracy or adequation but by way of the shadowed emergence of the ontological difference between being and beings.[60]

The *lived experience* of being Black is the existence of the jarring impossibility of questioning, of that anti-subject who can only be Human by problematizing the form of the Human.

The lived experience, Moten goes on, is what it is 'to be an irreducibly disordering, deformational force while at the same time being absolutely indispensable to normative order, normative form'.[61] What Moten reveals here is that the White supremacist, normative regime of modernity relies on this impossible logic that is *the lived experience* of being Black.

Previous studies of this difference between the *lived experience* and the *fact* of Blackness, such as Martiniquais psychiatrist and philosopher Frantz Fanon's, had seen the gap between them as a shift from being *things* to being *objects*. Fanon encounters himself as an 'object in the midst of other objects', observed and framed by a White way of seeing that freezes him, disabling the possibility of his own position as a seeing subject in the world.[62] Moten, however, is in pursuit of a fugitive slippage between these two positions, beyond the thing and before the object. 'I wish to engage a kind of pre-op(tical) optimism in Fanon that is tied to the commerce between the lived experience of the black and the fact of blackness and between the thing and the object—an optimism recoverable, one might say, only by way of mistranslation,' a mistranslation that begins in Fanon as his English translators render the famous fifth chapter of *Black Skin, White Masks*—which in the original French is 'L'expérience vécue du Noir'—as 'The Fact of Blackness', where 'The lived experience of the Black' would be more fitting.[63]

Between those resolute moments, Moten finds a process of Blackness that is always in escape, always moving out of the capturing frameworks of the *fact* and the *lived experience*. There is an 'ensemble', a 'stolen, transplanted organ', as he calls it, at work in the *excess* of the juridical scenes of normative forms.

The normative functions of (White) society and (White) law are founded on the possibility of objectifying a certain form of life, life that is too dark for the visual optics of this genocide, but *before* that objectification occurs—before the moment of the *thing* becoming an *object*—another *ontological* mode has escaped, fugitively, in what Cedric Robinson calls—as I talk about more below—the 'ontological totality', or what Moten calls 'para-ontology', the form of the form of life; the superstructure of belief in (Black) life that precedes and exists in excess of the lived experience of being Black.

'Moreover,' Moten writes, 'the brutal history of criminalization in public policy, and at the intersection of biological, psychological, and sociological discourse, ought not obscure the already existing ontic/ontological criminality of/ as blackness.'[64] The *life* of Blackness exists already as a form of collective belief, an undercurrent of antecedent ontologies, that precedes the lived experience of Black *lives*.

Fred Moten is not an Afropessimist. He began a way of thinking called Black optimism, one of the other branches of the broader set of radical investigations called Black studies, or the Black radical tradition. It is in this view of the *life* of Blackness preceding and exceeding the *lives* of Blackness that Moten diverges from the thinking of Afropessimists.

English Black studies scholar David S. Marriott brings this distinction to contemporary political movements. The Black Lives Matter movement is, obviously, for the broad liberation of Black *lives*. Marriott sees this as misguided, somewhat, since the liberal agenda of 'mattering' can only achieve the status of mattering within the racist and property-possessive logics that code Black social *lives* as Black social *death*. Being focused on *lives* over *life* allows for easier appropriation of the group's radicalism into the White-centred liberal politics of the state's normative function. Now 'Black Lives Matter' is part of the scripted ideology of government officials and state institutions. And once the university or the government say something, that something has been killed.

Marriott discusses this through his theory of 'corpsing', which builds on the theatrical term that refers to the moment when an actor blunders their lines or slips from their function of upholding fiction. The actor makes a mistake, diverting from the prescribed format of maintaining fictional lines, and the response is laughter. The extra scenes after movies that show the actors failing to perform are the 'corpsing' scenes.

Marriott is interested in how the inability to properly perform a social function becomes so unbearable to an audience that laughter is the only way of responding to corpsing. The corpse is too absurd to endure.

Marriott notes that corpsing exists also outside of theatre. In any situation where a prescribed social role is mis-performed by exceeding the coordinates given to the role, corpsing occurs. Those who obey their social roles are seen as subjects, as agents; while those who fail to perform are corpses.[65]

Black lives in this era of racial capitalism are, Marriott says, 'lived under the command of death', descended from slavery and subject to constant state-enforced brutality. The prescribed social performance of Black lives is social death. So what is it to corpse a Black performance? Is it the death of death? The 'relation of race to corpsing is one where the subject fails to escape its socially dead conception'.[66]

Corpsing is the 'knowledge and loss of the rules determining the subject',[67] but Black *life* is the position of the anti-subject in racial capitalism, or the visuality of modernity. Marriott defines this, through the 'condition of the slave', as Black life under the ownership of another, which is therefore forced to perform the role of social death in which life itself—juridically, socially, politically recognized and sovereign life—is the paramount impossibility. When a Black person *corpses*, then, she emerges as *social life*, against and in excess of the prescribed performance that regulates her death.

> Since the slave cannot easily play the role of a legal person… it follows that as society establishes, recognizes, and assumes the racial rights of citizenship, the black subject must confront the discomforting possibility that any performance of black social life is always corpsed by the fact that racial blackness is seen to be the performance of radical indebtedness or loss. The sum of black being, therefore, and its highest power is to know itself as a mortgaged claim on the living—that is, blacks must learn not to speak or perform life nor to desire this role.[68]

The act that renders possible the ontological escape of Black *life* is the rejection of the performance of lives, which is already coded as social death. The social form of lives that is called Black in racial capitalism is necessarily a dead social form. The *death of death*—the sociality of the ontological totality, that undercurrent sound that connects the islands of the undercommons—is the antecedent resistance of *Black life*. That's what this is about.

In *Queen & Slim*, there is no pursuit of social life. The protagonists do not attempt to exonerate themselves for the blessing of the law, nor to excuse their acts for the mercy of the police and the courts. From the very moment of their fugitivity, they know that this fugitive condition preceded their lives. The *social life of social death* came long before they began their date, or their lives. They have no interest in reconciling themselves within the framework of the law and the racial capitalist state of America. Instead, they focus on their internal meaning, the fugitive language that opens in the space of an already-given function of death.

By the end of the film, they will be murdered by many police officers at once. That final scene is also, in a ghostly temporality, the first scene. They are already murdered, by the entire logic that is the police force, by its every individual performer and by its institutional logics of anti-Black genocide.

The police only have any real presence at minor moments in the film, and each is pervaded by a Black operation beneath the visual surface, which Professor Cedric Robinson—the canonical historian of Black studies—would call the *ontological totality*.

The *ontological totality* is the meaning of meaning, the feeling of feeling, the Black language of Black reason beyond the grasp of normative visuality. As Robinson writes, what endures in Black *life* is 'the continuing development of a collective consciousness informed by the historical struggles for liberation and motivated by the shared sense of obligation to preserve the collective being, the ontological totality'.[69]

This 'shared sense of obligation' that vibrates beneath the visual surface is what occurs constantly in *Queen & Slim*. When Queen and Slim are almost caught while staying at a White couple's house, a Black police officer goes looking for the source of a noise he heard in the garage. Outside of view, beyond the reason of the White officers, the Black man hears an undercurrent of the scene. The ontological totality connects the pursuits throughout history, 'the continuing development of a collective consciousness'. The Black police officer finds the fugitives, and lets them go.

In another scene, Queen and Slim are getting their car fixed at a garage and Slim calls his parents. His father answers, and they say they love each other, but just when Slim is about to confess where he is headed, his father hangs up. The father's surroundings are revealed. His living room is full of White police officers, who berate him for hanging up. He refuses to aid their search.

The White police do not appear again until they emerge as murderers in the final scene. Even there, as they shoot repeatedly, Queen and Slim fall into the shape of a cross, Queen lying perpendicular to Slim, dead across his lifeless chest. The ontological totality of Black Christianity—the belief beyond the reach of the state's regulating reason—has endured the repeated scene of the kill.

The scriptwriter Lena Waithe, as I mentioned earlier, says that the film is not 'anti-cop' but is an attempt to '*humanize* Black people' in order to stop the current 'open season on Black bodies'.

But to *humanize* Black life is necessarily anti-cop. If Black life is Human life, then the police as an institutional logic is rendered obsolete. The police exists to regulate the border between *Black* life and *Human* life. The life drive and the undercommon (Black island) language of the characters open another form of life, a sociality that speaks and exists otherwise, in the ontological totality, and that form of life is the anti-logic that breaks the methodology of racist social organization that *is the police*. The humanization of the ontological totality is the rupture of the normative social form, especially—as it is in *Queen & Slim*— when it is conducted beneath and beyond the operation of visuality, with characters speaking outside of sight, contacting each other's emotive consciousness beyond the reach of the audience's gaze.

I get the feeling that *Queen & Slim* is the first film I have seen about Black *life*, rather than Black *lives*. Because the thing is this: Black people talking to each other beyond the logics of visuality *is anti-cop*. The police regulates the optics of race, and Black island languages ruin that regulation. And that is a pretty radical thing, which also means a pretty beautiful thing.

* * *

Ah, the sound of water beneath boats, Idi. The sound of an impossible visuality. The island noise of the endless water, obscured beyond its appropriation as the universal and homogeneous Sea.

*   *   *

I think about my love of Jasbir Puar's idea of the debilitation of racialized, queered, and trans bodies. She makes the argument against racialization so much more complex, so much more specific.

And sometimes at night, Idi, when I'm walking home from the Institute of Maritime Images, Etc., and thinking about all the horrible things I've seen, all the violence we've watched together on Instagram, I wonder about the debilitation of fish. Would the hunters and Fishing Girls catch the fish if they didn't have to pierce and puncture it first?

When they go fishing, they have a hook on a line. The fish moves towards the line and its face is punctured by the sharp hook. It is stuck on the line because the line is made for piercing skin, for shifting scales. And then they drag it up and hold it, the trophy's trophy.

But Idi, would they catch the fish if it wasn't debilitated by its punctured flesh? Is its debilitation the condition of its capture? By puncturing its flesh, the fish is categorized as naturally inferior to the (fishing/hunting) Human who is not punctured. The Human is whole, with no hook through its mouth.

Teasingly, the Human puts piercings in its ears and eyebrows and nose and nipples, just to laugh at how removed it is from vulnerability to being pierced.

The fish is defined by being vulnerable to piercing, and that becomes its nature. It is *natural* that fish get holes in their faces. Nature is a narrative that justifies the puncturing of fish.

We put holes in fish, Idi, so putting holes in fish is what we're supposed to do.

Fish can swim so quickly, so smoothly through the resistance of salty water.

And *female artists*, Idi—despite their hysteria, the holes in their bodies, their vulnerability to being punctured—are capable of two things at once, the genius of multitasking in spite of it all. That's what I've heard. Been told that all my life, forever.

* * *

If someone discovers your nuclear secrets, says Nina Simone, you'll wish you were dead.[70] But what if someone discovers your fishing fantasies were that *the fish catches you*? You won't wish you're dead. You'll wish the camera was off. A more terrifying proposition than death, possibly: to be unfilmed, uncaptured in the course of the spectacle, left behind like some unhooked fish who didn't even have the wherewithal to grab the hanging treat and pose on a boat, which is, after all, *its nature.*

* * *

The thing about men, Idi, is that we are always constituted within property. To be a *man* is to have a certain kind of relation to property. We *manage* property. Some of us *inherit* property. We *exchange* and *accumulate* property, in many forms. Wives, houses, capital.

The first ever representation of (male) masturbation in literature is about property.

In the Hebrew Bible's Genesis, Onan (38:8-9) does not want to 'raise up seed' with his dead brother's widow because in Deuteronomic law (which is the Law of Judaism; Deuteronomy, 25:5-10) the brother of the dead man must have a child with the widow, whose child then inherits the property of the dead man *and* the dead man's brother. If Onan agreed, he would have lost his property, so 'it came to pass, when he went in unto his brother's wife, that he spilled it on the ground, lest that he should give seed to his brother' (King James Version).

The white waste of his pleasure, of every man's pleasure, always carries that symbolic spatial domination. The man's white pleasure leaks out materially, occupying space, and this spatializing action that pauses time—the brief calm after ejaculation, before the body-war begins again—reflects back onto the man's white mind.

Onan cums on the ground to protect his house, and his possession of the women in his house.

But that act of protection, that patriarchal machine of violence disguised as protection, is always self-abolishing. The violence of the spill is soaked back into the ground; the barriers of protection collapse on the inhabitants.

Directly after Onan's masturbatory moment, he is killed in the style of the God of Genesis, with his famously unforgiving bluntness: 'And the thing which he did displeased the LORD, wherefore he slew him also' (Genesis, 38: 10).

* * *

For Black feminist philosopher Jennifer C. Nash, it is of course true that visuality—the visual regime of modernity—is built on racializing violence. The history of numerous visual technologies, including the Human body itself, is necessarily entwined with the racial imperative of capitalist modernity that tries to homogenize life into simple signifying coordinates for the purpose of supremacy and profit; coordinates like Black = Slave, White = Master; Woman = servile, Man = dominant. The trend in critiques of visual culture 'demonstrates both that representation is a practice which consistently makes demands on black women to expose their imagined differences and that representation is a racialized practice because visual technologies—most notably the photograph—emerged, at least in part, to make imagined racial and sexual difference visible'.[71]

The problem that Nash keeps coming up against is not the intention of the critique, but rather that it 'collectively *presumes the meaning of the black female body* in the visual field and assumes that representation injures black women'.[72] There is the violent current of visuality and its codes of representation that configure life according to proximity to vulnerability, but all of this misses out the autonomous experience of having a Black body, and what kinds of pleasure and ecstasy can be gained through that.

Nash knows that beyond and beneath the hegemonic plane of violence, there is a Black space—an island as a different way of living to the dominating Sea—where a kind of ecstasy is attainable that couldn't be known without this particular and disjunctive relationship to representation.

This kind of ecstasy is deeply, fugitively connected to what Fred Moten thinks of as Black optimism. The operations of seeing and thinking, for Moten, 'are driven by a nocturnal logic in which it is understood that absence, darkness, and death corrode and that black bodies are such corrosion's agential sign, held tightly within the sensual register and regulation of in/visibility'.[73] What it is to be Black is what it is to be the carrier of the unregulated feeling of darkness, the nocturnal logic of fear. That is the oppressive side.

But there is also an *optimistic* side, precisely as Black optimism. 'Blackness is the nonexcluded middle with a right to (refuse) philosophy. This unruly, performing, gestural, postinaugral apparatus of the logic of modernity moves in the form of a kind of hope and a kind of reassurance.'[74] Blackness is also the nodal point right in the centre of everything, because what our White supremacist polite schooling doesn't tell us is that the very politics and poetics of daytime—that are so happy about their cohering and logical languages—secretly rely on the *incoherence of the night*. Within that incoherence, within that catachrestic sound that means exactly nothing to the frameworks of language we have learnt forever, there is Nash and her ecstasy, and Moten and his optimism.

In Nash's reading of canonical Black feminist scholar Hortense J. Spillers, the *sound* of this fugitive movement is crucial. In the visuality of capitalist modernity, 'race is constituted by a repeated sadistic white pleasure in black female suffering'.[75] From the proto-scientific experiments with enslaved Black women's bodies in the eighteenth and nineteenth centuries,[76] to the European fascination with Black women's bodies on display (such as the 'Hottentot Venus', Saartjie Baartman), to contemporary online pornography, 'the pleasurable production of racial difference for white subjects, and the infliction of racial brutality on black female flesh, is a quintessentially visual practice'.[77]

For Spillers, the visual field is impossible as a locus for liberation. It is already constituted within the racializing violence of the Sea, of its violent way of looking that informs and constructs its racist way of knowing.

Instead, Spillers engages with the sonic field as an alternative and fugitive language for Black female subjectivity. The internal ecstasy of the Black female (or *feminized*) body contains a language that can signify something totally antagonistic and alternative to the normative frameworks of racializing visuality. Gathering that Black female subjectivity and withdrawing it into a fugitive groundwork of liberation is a process that Nash calls 'recovery work'.

Nash's favoured recovery work—diverging from Spillers' focus on sound—is concerned with Black women's visual imaginings of Black female subjectivity itself. She remains inside the visual field, but turns inwards, towards self-portraiture and archival referencing, surrounding the site of oppressive visibility with the noiseful opacity of a Black island language.[78]

The point here at the Institute of Maritime Images, Etc., is not to choose between Spillers and Nash. It is to listen for that ecstatic sound that escapes in the song and the self-portraiture of Blackness, of its fugitive roots that circle inwards.

That's the space that I think of as an island, Idi, in case you were wondering, hand-on-chin in the concentrated archipelago.

* * *

Japanese novelist and man concerned—as one should be—with sex and houses, Jun'ichirō Tanizaki thought about most objects in his life that 'again we have to come off the loser for having borrowed'.[79] The Japanese prefer 'a pensive luster to a shallow brilliance', dirty tin plates to the polished and shined Western silver, and to 'preserve and even idealize' the darkness and dirt of life rather than the Westerners who prefer to 'expose every speck of grime and eradicate it'.[80]

While Tanizaki was growing up in the early twentieth century, Japanese culture was gradually cast into the expanding Sea of Western homogeneity. Everything was becoming the same. He went to a restaurant once, while writing his book of essays praising shadows, and electric lights were turned up brightly. He asked where all the candles had gone, which had kept the place in semidarkness for as long as he could remember. The staff mumbled about some American fad; bright lighting, hard scrubbing.

It was not so much that every moment and material of Japanese life was being rendered into an American form, but that the objects were made to be used in the specific rituals of Euro-American culture. The electric lights and shined silver cutlery were aesthetically incompatible with the feeling and experience of being Japanese. Electric heaters, glass windows, papers, pens, and even the alphabet were being subsumed into a rolling Euro-American tide that didn't fit the practices of

Japanese life.

The particular way of life that makes being Japanese meaningful was becoming lost. Tanizaki's is not a conservative and luddite complaint.[81] It is a remark of self-preservation against homogenization. *Globalization* meant—and means—becoming American, and becoming American means becoming (or failing to become) a White and property-owning capitalist.

Tanizaki takes even the fundamental matter of life as involved in this process. Normative physics, chemistry, and biology are discourses imposed by Euro-American institutions, not by Japanese ways of thinking the matter, chemicals, and life of earth. He asks:

> how different everything would be if we in the Orient had developed our own science...would not the techniques and industries based on [modern sciences] have taken a different form, would not our myriads of everyday gadgets, our medicines, the products of our industrial art...have suited our national temper better than they do?[82]

Would there be a physics of the island, an island chemistry? If the Japanese island had fully resisted the dominating project of the Sea, what ways of knowing would be accessible to the island life of earths? What unimaginable languages would be speakable to forms of islands?

How much we could know if everything wasn't the same.

* * *

The bikini was supposedly invented by French engineer and designer Louis Réard, and named by him after Bikini Atoll in the Marshall Islands. The USA turned the atoll into a nuclear test site in the 1940s and 50s, evacuating its entire population. A book about the history of the bikini was published in 2012, written by

Patrik Alac. While Idan the Man will not disclose his sources, some of the photographs at the Institute of Maritime Images, Etc., on Instagram come from *Sports Fishing* magazine, where a photographer called Hunter Ledbetter has a section called 'Sports Fishing Girls', which resulted in the compilation 'Sports Fishing Girls Favorites' in April 2015. Ken Schultz describes his website as the place for 'Independent, Comprehensive, Authoritative Sportfishing Information'. Vladimir Putin takes his shirt off to catch fish with his dangling Rod, dipped longly into a lake in Siberia. He also brings a film crew.

What do these people have in common? They are all excluded from a certain way of being known as the *'female artist'*, or 'Woman'.

The parallels between this type of framed Human called 'Woman' and Bikini Atoll in the Marshall Islands are quite strange.

Bikini is uninhabitable because of heavy nuclear testing at the beginning of the Cold War, resulting in dangerously high levels of radioactive isotopes in the water. Women, also, are understood as uninhabitable (*no one understands women*) because of a long history of heavy misogynist testing: burning on the pyre, drowning, not-paying, beating, raping, murdering.

The islands were chosen as the site of nuclear testing by warmongering men who ventured out to sea to perform the kill. The etymology of the islands' name supposedly describes a German colonial appropriation of the Marshallese name *Pikinni*, coming from the parts *'pik'*, which means *surface*, and *'Ni'*, meaning *coconut*. The group of islands in the middle of the sea are called the *surface coconut*.

Men drift out on the Sea of their universal bodies to find two things in bars: breasts, which are represented in Renaissance theatre by men with coconut halves on their chests, and frothing surfaces, which sit on the tops of pints of beer.

Certain kinds of people who sometimes have the capacity

to internally reproduce other people were chosen as the site of misogynist testing by people who were desperate for something to photograph while at Sea. The Sea cannot infinitely expand, Idi, without the technology of visuality to push out its way of seeing. It must turn the earth into a singular World seen by Men.

To know what Bikini Atoll itself feels about being the namesake of a certain level of clothing, a certain category of body, is difficult. In my hegemonic body-form, I cannot speak to islands. I do not understand their undercommon language.

So maybe we can ask instead why *female artists* want to wear bikinis on yachts while killing fish.

There are some barriers to accessing this form of knowledge that *female artists* have. For one thing, I am Man, as you can see, and that requires a certain epistemology, a certain oppressive signifying function. By being Man, I assume and continue the assumption that there is some coherence between bodies and social codes, between reproductive capacity and behavioural traits: by being 'Man' I also claim myths like 'masculinity' and 'maleness' and 'manliness'. I affirm some kind of connection between behaving and gendering, which there is no way of proving or justifying, but is nonetheless what our misogynist economy is built on.

Another barrier to discovering why *female artists* like going fishing and getting photographed is that I am not the only Man. Many other people also call themselves Men, and those Men have already processed the information available to me through their own oppressive signifying functions. For example, when you type 'fishing women' into Google, the first suggested question is, 'How do you get a girl to go fishing?' which presumes that the Man has the fishing agency; Man is the killer, and it is his job to convince the unwilling Woman (or 'girl' in Men's fishing dialect) to do what he wants: kill some bodies and photograph other bodies in bikinis.

* * *

It is certainly, imminently, possible to know how the Bikini Islanders feel about their removal from home, and the use of their home as a bomb-testing range. On 1 March 1954, the largest weapon the USA has ever tested was exploded on Bikini Atoll. As the Bikini Atoll website states, 'At 15 megatons, the blast vaporized 3 islands and was 1,000 times the magnitude of the Hiroshima and Nagasaki nuclear weapons dropped on Japan in World War II.'[83]

When testing began in 1946, the 167 Bikini Islanders living on the atoll were moved some 700 kilometres away to Kili Island, also in the Republic of the Marshall Islands. In 1970, 100 residents were repatriated; however the contamination was so dangerous that they were removed again by 1980. Now the atoll is only occupied occasionally by researches and caretakers.

The American military convinced the Bikini Islanders to leave by stating the use of their home as a nuclear testing site was 'for the good of mankind and to end all world wars'. The Bikinian leader—King Juda—agreed, assured that they would be able to return to their home shortly. Most of them would never return, and many are still seeking repatriation and rights to their land today. The latest appeal to the US Congress was in 2018.[84]

The USA replaced the Bikini Islanders with a huge ensemble of military weapons and machines, alongside 5400 rats, pigs, and goats to test their devices on.

Before the Americans arrived, the atoll was colonized by Japan. Before that it was under the colonial rule of Germany, and before that—since its military first sailed there from Europe in the seventeenth century—by Spain. The Japanese military built a fort on Bikini to protect against American invasion during World War II, which eradicated the Bikinian way of life.

The Americans did invade, however, capturing the Marshall

Islands' Kwajelein Atoll in 1944. On Bikini, there were five Japanese soldiers left. They retreated to a hole, hiding from the spreading force of American weaponry, but there was nowhere else to go. Instead of being taken as prisoners of war, compacted into the service of their enemy, they exploded a grenade in their final hiding place, an act of suicide that robbed the new invader of its invading pleasures.

The US military moved the Bikini Islanders around as they shifted their explosive and extractive operations in the many islets and atolls of the Marshall Islands. In September 1948, some Bikinians were taken to Kili to begin clearing the land as a possible site of settlement, and the Bikinians on Kwajelein were moved there just 2 months later. On Kili, starvation was an acute problem for the Bikinians, as their traditional methods of making food on Bikini were no longer possible, and rough seas made it difficult to bring anything from other islands.

In 1979 the Marshall Islands gained independence from the USA, establishing self-government across its enormous archipelago. The US still has administrative control over the country, though. The USA is today the world's largest empire, with governing control of Puerto Rico, the Virgin Islands, Guam, the Northern Marianas, and American Samoa, and 'special responsibilities' for the Federated States of Micronesia, the Marshall Islands, and Palau, as Chamorro poet Craig Santos Perez writes.[85]

The people of these archipelagic territories of the USA do not have American rights, but their lives are regulated from the land that calls itself *continental* America, in opposition to the watery archipelagic separatedness of the *overseas territories*.

The US withdrew its military rule over the Marshall Islands in 1971, which also halted their regular flights between Kwajelein and Bikini, keeping the Bikinians even further from their homeland.

Guam—another nation under the administrative empire

of *continental America*, in the group of Pacific island countries called Micronesia—has similarly fought for centuries against colonization, has similarly been ignored as simply another island to use as a strategic point of command between the desired continents, has similarly been rejected as a logic and a life-form of its own and understood by continental empires solely as a means of extracting profit and appropriating populations on the continents either side of the ocean.

The islands are so broken up, so washed about in the flux of the sea, like narrative, like slices of poetry.

The islands are so tiny, so concentrated in their specificity.

So disconnected to whatever comes over them, before them, a thousand kilometres from their withdrawing shores.

In 2009, the USA and Japan proposed a new series of military constructions in Guam, filling up the small island with soldiers and the cascade of massive weaponry that follows them. The 11,000-page proposal was delivered and Chamorros—the people of Guam—were given 90 days to read it and respond. Among other things, as Santos Perez writes, it detailed 'how the military planned to build a live firing range complex around the ancient Chamorro village of Pågat, to replace hundreds of acres of jungle for permanent military facilities, and to rip out more than two million square feet of living coral reef to dredge a deep-draft wharf'.[86]

Chamorro poet Melvin Won Pat-Borja responded, as poets do, as Chamorros do, with poetry:

Sir, what if we protest and unite as a people, and in the end they just do whatever they want?

I understand that the federal government has done worse things and gotten away with it, like smallpox blankets, like nuclear testing in the Marshall Islands, like dropping bombs on Vieques, like holding the sovereign queen of Hawai'i at gunpoint to sign the annexation.[87]

The Marshallese lawsuit against the USA for its invasion and mismanagement of the islands is brought by the Bikini, Kili, and Ejit local Marshallese governments, and seeks at least US$561,036,320. In 1975, a trust fund of $3 million was established by the US government for the Bikinians. When they were again removed from Bikini beginning in 1978, another $3 million was added to the trust fund. In 2006, this fund closed, which is when the lawsuit began.

The hands of your Presidents are drenched in the blood of our fallen—the same presidents that we are not allowed to vote for.[88]

In her *Pocket Atlas of Remote Islands*, German writer Judith Schalansky only mentions the Marshall Islands once—Taongi Atoll, specifically—and her story about it, in a book made of stories about islands, is not to do with the Marshall Islands itself, but rather about an American man who travels to Hawai'i and disappears on his boat, which then washes up years later on Taongi.[89]

In 2001, the Nuclear Claims Tribunal granted Bikinians $563,315,500, including a loss of value of $278,000,000, restoration costs of $251,500,000, and suffering and hardship value of $33,814,500. However, the Nuclear Claims Tribunal did not actually have the funds to pay this amount to Bikinians, forcing them to take this claim to the US Congress to convince them to pay.[90]

In her poem 'It's Time to Rise', Marshallese poet Kathy Jetñil-Kijiner calls the Marshalls 'the land of survivors', 'a country more sea than land'.[91] What it must take to survive that much Sea, that much movement into the squeezed concentrate of your island. The island is, slowly, inside the Sea. The video of Jetñil-Kijiner's poem shows construction machinery on a beach, grazing the final embers of industrial calories between the Sea and the land, before the distinction erodes and the poet herself is consumed, walking alone in a tiny strip, an archipelagic isthmus in its final throes, and its winding possibility of revival. 'Let me show you airports under water, bulldozed reefs, blasted sands, and plans to build new atolls, forcing land from an ancient, rising sea. Forcing us to imagine turning ourselves to stone.' The cities of empires will have to learn to breathe underwater, while these island lives are stuffed and set upon corpsing stones, the ridicule of the lifeless island form; positioned as a tourist outpost, as an archipelagic strategy to access conquerable continents; but these island lives know how to breathe, breathe underwater, because they are mostly water and they have been since before anyone remembers, since before the moment the Sea appeared, just there, behind them. Empire Cities will have to learn how to breathe like islands, or the survival trained in these closed archipelagos will go, down into the Sea where everything looks exactly the same; it's bloated and it's dead and blue. 'My sister, I offer you these rocks as a reminder that our lives matter more than their power,' says Greenlandic Inuit poet Aka Niviâna to Jetñil-Kijiner, offering her a basket of rocks. And they say together, 'each and every one of us has to decide if *we will rise*'.[92] To *rise* is a threat from inside the Sea, it seems, but the island lives of Jetñil-Kijiner and Niviâna appear as the possibility of an island *rising out* of the Sea, emerging again as an island, as the land of survivors, where many may have been swept away in their fight against the Sea, many may have been subsumed into the military operations of transoceanic warfare, but their form survived, the form that is their survival. And that form is given in the rocks that will rise from the Sea, while the Cities of Empire continue to watch the sprawling upwards motion of the tide on TV screens, hooked on the bait of expansion. The island is rising, coming back again as an island, forming archipelagic links only with other islands, living as resistance to the project of the Sea.

Let the record show that in the face of oppression and injustice, the people of Guam refuse to live a life absent of liberty, that we refuse to accept anything less than justice, that we refuse to sell Guam to the highest bidder. And should we die fighting your war machine, let your history books show your children the struggle that we fought to find freedom in a country filled with hypocrisy. Let the record show that Guåhan stood up and said, Uncle Sam, sorry, but No Deal.[93]

* * *

I go looking for info, Idi. I find an article about *fishing women* on the World-Famous and Highly Renowned FishingBooker blog by a Man named Sean with no surname. In the article, mononymous Man Sean refers to *female artists* as *female anglers*, which I presume is just a continued misspelling of *female artists*, unless King Sean hasn't been listening to anything we've said at the Institute of Maritime Images, Etc., but I can hardly believe that. Surely everyone knows by now. *Especially the Men.*

Among the *female anglers* is Fishie Manson (name changed for anonymity), who is photographed with what seems to be a very small baby Human with no arms and no legs and green scales instead of skin. Where she found such a person, and why she is holding it dead in her arms with such a big smile on her face, is a mystery to me.

Weirdly, Fishie Manson has no gills, no spinal dorsal fin, no soft dorsal fin, no lateral line, no anal fin, no spiny rays, no caudal fin, no air bladder, no pelvic fin, no pyloric caeca, and can't even breathe in water. In fact, she barely seems to be a fish at all.

The other animals interviewed are Gonna Drown, who is 'one of the most influential fishing women in North America', whatever that means; Precision Female Stranglers, which seems to be some kind of murder cult; Fishing Women Competitively, which manifests as rusty cents in the bottom of the Trevi Fountain but is actually a series of puppet-strings that manipulate the global flow of spacetime; and Deadly Chokey, who has 'an infectious love' for fish blood and tackle, which she is very proud of. Scandalously, none of these fish is wearing a bikini, and yet they have all been photographed.[94]

I'm confused and tired, Idi. I need a break from the Institute. Goodnight.

* * *

Beauty has an upholding function, an architectural duty that constructs the frame for subjectivity. Certain kinds of subjectivity are maintained by the labour of their attendant beauty. I suppose you remember, Idi, how Vasari describes Brunelleschi. His ugliness in spite of his beautiful buildings. But let's not talk about that now. It's time for tea, as they say *at home [TAKE ME BACK TO DEAR OLD BLIIIIIGHTY]*. Ciao.

* * *

Writing about Black studies and feminism, about Blackened and feminized life, is a bit of a weird and risky passion when you're a White Man. There are several things about it, Idi.

I know lots of academics who study lots of different things. Not one of them gets asked *why* they study their subject *every time* they say what their subject is. One of my best friends, the legendary cider-pourer of Asturias Carlos Lozano, is a biologist. No one wonders why he chose to study marine biology. It is just accepted, throughout cultural norms, that an intelligent Spanish man may choose to study the evolution of fish.

Other friends are philosophers, literary critics, geographers, and legal scholars, and none of them is asked to justify their choices. And when Black people study Black studies, everyone knowingly nods, as if that is the only thing that a Black scholar could ever have been interested in researching. But when you're White and in Black studies, everyone demands to know *what the hell you are thinking?!*

In my experience, strangely, it's mostly White people who react negatively to the notion of a White person being involved in Black studies, but it's mostly women who react negatively to the notion of a man being involved in feminism. Although it's hard to remember *every* conversation, I think that every time I have spoken to a Black person about what I study, it has seemed quite clear and obvious to them that this is a very important area of research, so why not study it? This is also the case for other non-White people. Whereas lots of times I have spoken to White people about it, they seem very confused. It doesn't seem like a real subject to them. One friend even informed me, 'It seems a bit...*racist*—it's called *Black studies*, which kind of excludes White people.'

I wanted to say that every other subject in schools and universities is preceded by the word *White*, it's just not written on the curriculum—there are degrees in *White engineering*, *White anthropology*, *White film studies*, *White economics*, *White marine biology*—but it wouldn't have helped, so I held it in.

I think a lot of this comes from a confusion between *lives* and *life*, which is to say, between *politics* and *ontology*. People are shocked at the thought that I—a very obviously White Man, all pale and balding and blotchy—write about *Black lives* and *feminized lives*. They presume that I am actively involved in antiracist and feminist political movements. But those things are all *political*.

It's not that I disagree with political movements and political action. Over the years, I have been involved in parts of that, and—despite a reticence to overtly make the claim while not actively involved in the struggle—I still consider myself a communist anarchist. It's more that what I am concerned with is the *ontological condition* that is the raciality of modernity. Before any lives exist, before the experience of being alive, the permanent and antecedent condition of modernity is the *racialization* and the *gendering* of all life. Life as ontology — as the condition of the meaning of life, the possibility of such a thing as 'life' coming into being — is categorized into various social referents, which denote proximity to violence. *That* is beyond and before politics, and that is what I study.

The political claim is that *Black lives matter*. The ontological response is not that *Black life matters* or *does not matter*, but rather that *Black life is not matter*. It is an immaterial structure of belief, a fugitive operation that exceeds the lived experience of lives. It is supremely *social*, not physical. Fred Moten, with his typically astounding precision, calls this the 'animaterial, metaphysical thing in itself that exceeds itself'.[95]

* * *

So how *do* you get a girl to go fishing, boys?

There are numerous stages to the operation.

1. You must initiate a binary system of bodily signification in which a body that looks more or less reproductive equals weakness/hysteria/unwillingness and a body that looks more or less non-reproductive equals strength/rationality/willingness. This step may take a few centuries, so plan long in advance of the fishing trip, preferably by several generations.

2. You need to shift the strict binary performance of your new misogynist economy in order to convince people that Men are the ones who do the convincing, while Women are the ones who get convinced. Do this by setting up a liberal framework of quotable phrases (TOP TIP: print them on T-shirts and books that Men own and Men make profit from!), which produces the appearance of difference within the binary system. Some

Women will choose to associate with a set of behaviours called 'feminine', and others will choose a set called 'masculine', all on a scale of severity. Men, also, will position themselves along the scale. Now the World of Men appears to be much more complex than Men-work and Women-make-babies. Now *a girl* will be set up for believing the possibility of deciding to go fishing.

3. Through interweaving mythologies, make the act of killing the only heroic achievement of the bodily pinnacle called 'Man'. Attempt to make this a global practice, so that various disconnected cultures all produce literature that celebrates the scene of the kill. Over time, give this a sacrificial social function, making murder necessary for the maintenance of any group. This, also, could take millennia, so prepare lots of sandwiches before beginning.

4. At home, practise using your rod. Dip it into various fishing holes, and repeat the action of tossing it in. Make sure you are an expert of the rod, so much so that the rod is your point of access to the World.

5. Find *a girl*. Temporarily perform the set of behaviours called 'feminine', hugging and kissing her. Play repeated films and programmes in which Killers/Men are romantic before revealing their heroic Killer Instinct. Gradually reveal yourself as the Killer/Man.

6. Make sure to be born into a bourgeois family that has accumulated the value of violence and refused over generations to share it, instead forming a barrier of coagulating capital around itself as a series of endlessly expanding commodities. Make sure that one of these commodities is a boat. Ask Bourgeois Daddy for the boat, and take it in a car to the place where *a girl* lives. Show her Daddy's boat. In order to successfully merge the numerous behaviours that *convince a girl*, make sweet and gentle love beside Daddy's boat, while throwing knives at a tree and grunting.

7. Make sure you receive a car big and powerful enough to

carry a boat for your birthday *before* beginning the operation of getting *a girl* to go fishing (and especially before Point 6). If Daddy says *No* to this birthday car (TOP TIP: smash his rod if he refuses!), invest your surplus capital in extractive technologies just enough to accumulate a profit sufficiently large to buy a car on credit, but sufficiently small that everything is not extracted, which would flood the Sea with black oil and kill the fish before you (and *a girl*) get to them.

8. While sucking on the same string of spaghetti and rubbing *a girl*'s leg (and revving motorbike engines with your spare hand), tell *a girl* that you love killing fish. Remind her subtly that the scene of the Kill is heroic. All Men must Kill. While *a girl* is washing up the spaghetti plates, fuck your enemy's mother at the same time as you twist your enemy's nipples until he screams.

9. Drive to the Sea, towing Daddy's boat. Remove Daddy's boat from Daddy's car, and place it on the Sea. Gaze at the horizon (TOP TIP: make sure she notices this; and tense your pecks!) with distant assurance, letting her know that you are an expansive form of subjectivity, just like the Sea, and that is why you are a convincing Man. Try to speak in a baritone.

10. Growl and shoot your pistol into the air while you soothingly steer the boat into open waters.

11. Find a fishing hole to stick your rod in. If this all goes smoothly, *a girl* will offer you her own fishing hole to stick your rod in, which ultimately was the purpose of the previous ten steps of the operation.

12. Hook its mouth, drag it from its home, convince it that you (Man) are in fact the owner of its ocean-home since all the earth and the ocean is one single World and Sea, then penetrate its body with your knife, opening it up to the logics of your killer-sight, then kill it. Once it is dead, retroactively write the history so that you (Man) were the one who set up this entire scene and saved everyone from themselves. And as for the fish,

you can catch that too.

* * *

In English we like to say that we do not gender nouns. We gawp at the masculine sun of Spanish, and its feminine moon. We ridicule Italian's lady-tables and the genitals given their opposite gender. But everything in English is gendered, too, without the need for an *a* or an *o* on the end.

Architectural history is heavily invested in the masculinity of certain kinds of buildings. Andrea Palladio and his Palladian style are archetypally *masculine*. The most strictly neoclassical British architect who held to the principles of the Renaissance was Inigo Jones, even more formally classical than his contemporary Christopher Wren, who was more interested in mixing French and Italian Baroque in the style of the Counter Reformation.

Inigo Jones follows certain gendered procedures in his buildings: 'Ye outward ornaments oft to be sollid, proporsionable and according to the rulles, masculine and unaffected.'[96] The description perfectly presupposes the stance of the Kantian Enlightenment Man: all external stoutness, all emotional distance and calm removal, all masculinity and calculation.

Jones's St Paul's in Covent Garden, London is the figure of this feeling. Michael Levey defines it as 'masculine weight', in opposition to the spectacular intricacy of the Rococo style.[97]

British architects in general were suspicious of Rococo excess, instead developing their own kind of Protestant Baroque which Levey sites precisely in Oxford's early eighteenth-century Blenheim Palace, by John Vanbrugh. Otherwise they kept to the repeatable regularity of Georgian stuccoed fronts and rectangular symmetry, or 'masculine and unaffected' Palladianism.

One exception that gained a lot of criticism in the seventeenth century was Wren's St Paul's Cathedral on Ludgate Hill, London. Inigo Jones had worked on the repairs of the old medieval cathedral on the same site, with the same name, and Wren had taken over from him after the British Civil Wars of the 1640s, but in 1666 the whole thing burnt down in the Great Fire.

Wren designed a fully English Baroque replacement. Levey says that contemporary observers thought of it as too close to Francesco Borromini's 'wildly extravagant designs', making it a 'false and counterfeit Piece of Magnificence'.[98]

Masculinity here is not contrasted with femininity. Femininity is not even mentioned by Levey as the mode of Rococo extravagance and intricate, delicate Baroque beauty. The masculinity of Palladian geometry is contrasted with falsity, duplicity, fakeness. In these architectures between the Renaissance and the Enlightenment, what is not masculine is a lie.

This applies not only to architecture and the aesthetics of city designs, but also to people, to bodies. In Giorgio Vasari's *Lives of the Artists* — his sixteenth-century collective biography of Florentine artists, many of whom he knew personally — a simple and unassuming facade is given the semantic coordinates of reason.

A man who abides by strict geometrical principles and emotional disinterest is a real man. Vasari's description of Filippo Brunelleschi is exemplary:

There are many men whom nature has made small and insignificant, but who are so fiercely consumed by emotion and ambition that they know no peace unless they are grappling with difficult or indeed almost impossible tasks and achieving astonishing results. These men enhance and distinguish whatever they happen to take up, no matter how commonplace or worthless it may seem. So one may never look down one's nose at those who lack the fine grace and bearing with which nature should endow all artists when they come into the world; lumps of earth often conceal veins of gold. Men of unprepossessing appearance are very often magnanimous and pure in heart, and when nobility is added to their other qualities they may confidently be expected to work miracles. This can clearly be seen in the case of Filippo Brunelleschi; just like Forese da Rabatta and Giotto he was insignificant to look at, but his genius was so commanding that we can surely say he was sent by heaven to renew the art of architecture.[99]

The *insignificance* of looking at him is of great significance. The fact of his masculine purity means he is not worth looking at. Look, instead, at what he looks at.

The buildings that surround us in the city, in their history and their aesthetic meanings, affirm the binary feelings of gender. Big, bold, manly buildings, and frilly, Rococo, female excess. There is Reason and there is Hysteria written all over the walls of town.

The position of the *artist*, of the Photographer, is the position of architectural masculinity. The Photographer is always removed from the scene, disinterested, distanced, only involved through an artistic will that organizes the emotion of the scene; but the Photographer is never seen. What it means *to look* is already, always, deeply entangled in what it means to be *male*.

* * *

Ken Schultz describes himself in the same paragraph as both 'the absolute authority on sport fishing' and 'one of the foremost experts in sport fishing'. In his *Field Guide to Saltwater Fish*, he describes either fish shapes or fishing women shapes, without saying which.

[They have] uniquely evolved to suit the needs of their aquatic lives...Some are narrow, with bodies that are taller than they are thin...Some are flat, with bodies that are shorter than they are wide...Some are torpedo-shaped...Some are tubular...Shapes tend to be related to [the body's] habits and habitats. Narrow-bodied fish [or fishing women] are extremely maneuverable and tend to live in reefs or densely weeded ponds, where the ability to maneuver between rocks or plants is essential. Flatfish [or flat fishing women] tend to live on the bottom, where their low profiles prevent recognition. Torpedo-shaped fish [or fishing women] are built for speed and are found either in open water or in strong currents where less streamlined fish[ing women] would be swept away. Tubular fish[ing women] often live in small crevices and areas that are inaccessible to other animals [and men], rather than in wide-open ocean waters.[100]

What I want you to imagine for this part of the performance, Idi, is the life of a man named Ken Schultz who can force his own disappearance from the frame he looks at. This is only one of the two things he does. The other is writing long books about fish.

Ken Schultz, for legal reasons, is not a gilled aquatic craniate. He is, however, *authority*.

* * *

The *Urban Dictionary* gives various meanings of 'fishing'. The first is used in the phrase *fishing for compliments* and describes the moment 'when an obviously hot girl insults herself with the intention of having everybody around her disagree with what she said, triggering a barrage of compliments'.[101]

The second definition, which is maybe not so urban, is 'the process of tricking a fish into piercing its lip'. That is, 'the act of

fishing for fish'.
The third definition is:

> a strategy used by guys for picking up chicks on the beach in which one guy sends the stud in your group on a long bomb route and throws a football into a large group of hotties. The guy running the route will be forced to dive into the group to make the catch, thus landing face-first in the sand. The hotties will be both impressed by his remarkable athleticism and concerned for his safety. Your buddy will return to your beach house with the group of hotties, thus allowing you to pick off one of the looser chicks.

The final definition is when people who are under 18 or 21 stand outside a supermarket, asking adults to buy booze and/or cigarettes for them.

There is also a kind of 'fishing' used on dating apps. People 'fish' when they send out the same message to many people. If any 'bite the bait', then a selection ritual takes place. There are many magazine articles—all aimed at women, it seems—about avoiding this fishing practice.

I cannot find any articles, however, aimed at fish that warn of the dangers of fishing.

I have conflicted feelings about these meanings, about the social rituals of fishing. On some level, the only truly violent definition is that of traditional fishing itself—catching fish in water. It is murder, and it is an activity with no other goal than to kill. Somehow—maybe especially from my point of view as a lifelong vegetarian who has never eaten any meat or fish—it makes the other definitions seem trivial.

Fishing for compliments doesn't seem like anything untoward at all, despite the obvious disgust that the writer of the definition feels about what these 'obviously hot girls' do. Everyone likes being told nice things about themselves, so setting up a situation in which that happens doesn't seem so egregious. We all set up situations designed for our own pleasure constantly, so why shouldn't these marine survivors called 'obviously hot girls' do the same?

Every day, Idi, I set up an evening, and wait for the compliment of falling light, all for my own pleasure.

The stud/football/large group of hotties scene is more violent, more ritualistic, more prescribed and focused on the goal of the killing scene. It relies on strictly gendered assumptions about human behaviour: *female artists* will be impressed by displays of power, and have a tendency to care and nurture; *artists* will display power and be cared for while fishing. This all relies on a faulty methodology. It presumes a connection between random data. The first proposition is a leaping human with an erection; the second is the group's positive reaction; and the conclusion is some kind of sex fest. There is no connection between these stages, though.

The problem with that sandy-group/football stud fishing scene is not really the scene itself. There is nothing inherently violent about flirting, or contrived fantasy, or predictable mythologies of sexual satisfaction, or some people being impressed by what other people's bodies can do. There is, however, great violence in the presupposed narrative of natural and behavioural gender difference. The whole scene relies on the presumption that *female artists* or Fishing Girls will be a certain way, naturally, while Fishermen or *artists* will naturally be another way.

There is also, I suppose, violence in the disturbance of the scene itself. If the *female artists* sitting in a circle are interested in talking to each other, not in being disrupted by the jumping carrier of an unbearable erection, then there is violence.

The only solution to that, obviously, is to write a book about gender and fish and bikinis on Instagram, which will inevitably be the tolling bell of the revolution.

I met my fiancée, Genia, on a dating app, and I sent messages to lots of people I had matched with. The messages were either exactly the same or very similar. I didn't realize I was 'fishing', I just had nothing very interesting to say to people I had never met and knew nothing about. There was no context to our conversation, no mutual scene, so all the usual frameworks of conversation were removed.

I don't really know how violent that was, or how heavily it invested in the Sea's narrative of gendered binaries. The act of dating itself—its repetitivity, its endless evenings of precise repetition—removed any understanding from me of what was going on. I just went ahead, no idea why, because I vaguely conformed with a doctrine spoken universally that told me I will find something if I look. And, strangely, I did. I found the rest of my life in Genia.

Anyway, I wonder if cold women go fishing, Idi. All the definitions are about the hot ones.

* * *

Many early analyses of the visuality of pornography focus on the famed 'male gaze', which has since become a popular phrase of feminist discourse. At the Institute of Maritime Images, Etc., Idi, where women, men, fish, Instagram audiences, and other maritime and media animals are looking at trophies and murder, we cannot really rely on the idea that there is an established dominant gender doing the looking and an established submissive gender being looked at. Can there not be, as Nash asks, 'cross-sex identification' and more than the 'implicit normative judgment' of the singular male gaze?[102]

For one thing, Idi, I don't think we should presume that we are the first or the only people to take pleasure in viewing these bizarre hunting scenes, nor that anyone who takes pleasure from viewing them will share our social codes—one Jewish Israeli man, one White English man. By understanding ourselves as purveyors of the Male Gaze, we presume the universality of our way of looking. We presume that it's always Men—singular Men who are all the same—who look at Women in bikinis. While Patrik Alac tells me repeatedly that this is indeed the case, friends and heroes of mine are convinced that it is not.

For another thing, Nash's intention is really to shake the Black feminist archive into an internal language of ecstasy and desire that steps back from the archival 'preoccupation with injury and recovery' and instead opens a space 'for speaking about the complex ways that pleasure—both racial and sexual—moves under the skin'.[103] By focusing on the Male Gaze and the masculinized pleasure of pornographic visuality, and by imagining these racializing logics to be the singular scale of human perception, we foreclose the possibility of an island sound, an ecstasy of landed and fugitive sociality, beneath and beyond the homogenizing reach of the Sea's expanding project.

* * *

For me, Idi, study is the same as escape. I get this from my study of Black studies—I learn everything from my love of Black study.

To really *study* is to constantly try and *get out*, to escape and always be in the movement of escape, out of the expansive empire of the Sea. Study is an intentional communal activity, a way of getting together in whispered words with friends. It's the communist basement meeting, the gathering, the internal language of the island ensemble. Studying, for that reason and by that limitation, cannot be done in the university. The university is an anti-study machine. It sets prescribed directions for study. It inscribes maps of thought that guide students to an ever-expanding ocean of learning. It expects your knowledge to always grow, moving out like the Sea. That's anti-study.

The university only understands the process of thinking in relation to grades. A code is given to certain performances, and that establishes the student's position in relation to debt, which is the purpose of the university—creating debt, and expanding the profit-reproduction of debt, moving out like the Sea, turning everything wet, damp as debt, staining all life on earth with the mark of university debt, and the credit it awaits from us all.

While I write this book, Idi, having this conversation at the Institute of Maritime Images, Etc., I owe just over £70,000 to the British state. That is my reward for having successfully performed the ritual debt-dance of the university, three times over, from BA to PhD.

Studying, Idi, is about escape, escape within the limitations of the island. It's about staying dry, which means escaping from the expanding wetness of the Sea. That's what we do at the Institute of Maritime Images, Etc. We stay bone-dry like bones, Idi—like goddamn desert bones.

Universities are just soaking wet estate agencies, making debt and renting rooms.

* * *

I won't say much more today. I'll do something else in a little while. I'll take a break, a drink, and sit down over there. But I have a few more stories, if you've got the time.

* * *

The most creative thing I ever did was stand behind my local councillor and do everything he did in reverse. He stepped up onto the podium. I fell to the floor. He wrote a book of proclamations. I ate a book of empty pages. He went to the toilet. I jumped in the sewer. A little while into our game, he died of old age. Now I am condemned to live forever. That is the only act of creation I have ever achieved.

* * *

Patrik Alac's life achievements include 'published many articles in several German fashion magazines', and nothing else. He has also written two books about the bikini, which could very possibly be the same book: *The Bikini: A Cultural History*, and *Bikini Story*. In *Bikini Story*, he argues that books about history tend to focus on bad things: 'damage and destruction...wars and disasters'. He thinks people should write books about *good* things.

What's good, Idi? Bikinis.

The goodness of bikinis, for Alac, comes from the fact that they are the result of a history of liberalization. First, things are bad and people are oppressed. Then Christianity gets weaker and women show their bodies, uncovering them from cloth. Then, Patrik Alac writes a book with a thumbs up. And that's the twentieth century, basically.

Why would Alac dedicate his time to writing a book about bikinis? For one thing, he seems to live a world where everyone is permanently in a bikini. They are 'known and seen on a daily basis everywhere we go'.[104] Furthermore, he is not interested in bikinis on hangers, because they look like melted cheese stuck to the gratings in the oven, which is nothing like what he says.

> But on a woman, [the bikini] undergoes an incredible transformation to behold! Those two pathetic bits of cloth you might have thought were only accidentally on the shop's swimwear shelf suddenly change in form and dimension as if someone has breathed life into them. These patches of material on the skin are all at once points of interest, ornaments, even statements. The bikini reveals as much as

it clothes, an image which fills many male observers with enthusiasm at the sight of such a transformation.[105]

'Many male observers' is a long way of saying 'me'.

Alac says that it's *as if* someone has breathed life into bikinis. Like many men looking at women in bikinis, Patrik Alac is not quite aware of what he is saying when he speaks about women in bikinis. He is describing the difference between a bikini on a hanger and a bikini on a woman's body, a scene in which *life* is certainly given to the bikini. Why, then, is it only *as if* life was in them, rather than life *really* being in them? What inhabits the bikini is *like* life, but it is *not quite* life. It is recognizable as the movements of a living being, but it does not have the ability to disappear itself from the frame like real living things; things called 'male observers', of whom, Alac unknowingly warns, there are many.

Ken Schultz begins his book about seawater fish by putting their ability to 'breathe' in scare quotes. It is *as if* fish can breathe underwater. We humans — we many male observers of this Sea-World — know only one way of receiving oxygen into our bodies: breathing. Other things that do not breathe always seem to us *as if* they breathed, because that is the only point through which our understanding of survival with oxygen can be registered.

Fishing Girls exist in bikinis *as if* they were alive.

* * *

According to Patrik Alac — a man who has never worn a bikini but has spent his adult life looking at thousands of women in bikinis, just like another man called Elliot C. Mason (together they form the as-yet-unformed circus duo, *The Bikiidiots*) — everyone hated the sea and thought it was bloody horrible until the end of the nineteenth century when suddenly some women took some of their clothes off on 'aquatic recreational landscapes', which basically means beaches. Since then, everyone has been free and nothing bad has happened. Because of tits and stuff.

Tiffany Lethabo King has a slightly different take on history. While Patrik and I were at the beach bar Googling 'bikinis', King was writing a book called *The Black Shoals*.

In that book, King investigates how modern racialized subjectivity was constructed through and with the development of cartography in the early colonial USA. She builds multiple simultaneous propositions, each wound around complex networks of past and present phenomena, from eighteenth-century archives to King's daily drive into work.

As King reads through Brazilian philosopher of everything (race, modern sciences, spacetime, history, Latin American politics, gender...) Denise Ferreira da Silva, René Descartes established the European belief in two modes of human subjectivity: transcendent and affectable.

The *transcendent subject*, broadly, turns the world into the World of the Subject, transforming raw sensations from the earth's matter into Reason in the Human mind. The transcendent subject—called 'Man1' by Jamaican philosopher and writer Sylvia Wynter[106]—maps a single World according to the Human mind. The *affectable subject* is affected by the World, washed over by the Sea, and spatially designated by the *transcendent (European) subject*. The *affectable subject* is Black or Indigenous, and seen as both bound to nature and to the rule of *transcendent subjects*, which means European White Men.

When colonial Europeans arrive in what is now the USA, they try to impose a colonial cartographic grammar on those lands that they cannot yet understand as territory. They must mark clear and racialized lines of territory that designate proximity to nature.

Indigenous lives on the east coast are immediately marked out as open to natural manipulation; they are *affected* by their surrounding nature, and so they must be dominated by the European colonizers. It is precisely this seeming *nature* of Indigenous lives that creates such a brutal and genocidal drive towards the homogenization of cartography in the colonizers: the Indigenous people become markers of difference, and the only way of establishing a new White supremacist foundation, built on the transcendent subjects of a singular global cartography, is through the pursuit of the eradication of difference. Difference is used to justify its own extermination. As King writes, '[p] orosity and fungibility are elusive and difficult to visualize because they cannot be captured through traditional modes of seeing'.[107] The traditional mode of seeing to Europeans—what I have been calling *visuality*—is a framework that bulldozes everything in its way, using the logic of *race* to justify this constant and unending destruction.

European colonization is then a kind of flow from and as the Sea, breaking into the landed lives of Indigenous people and rendering them irrelevant and abolished in the singular spacetime of White modernity. However, this project keeps getting run aground, hitting into shoals of difference.

King reads US slave plantation maps on the Atlantic coast, which create a coastal semantics 'as a symbol of transition, flux, and uncapturability in a period in which the British colonies needed to put the landscape in motion to transform and conquer it'.[108] The land had to be *moved* in order for it to be fully exploited and its local population removed and killed, but something kept stopping the homogenizing movement of the Sea.

King calls that thing a shoal. The shoal is life that stops the encroachment of the Sea. It is a form of sociality that ruptures and stops the expanding movement of global ships and cartography. The amazing thing about the shoal is that its shoalness is based in its *difference*; it does not form a constitutive part of the homogeneous drive of the Sea—it is, archetypally, islandy. And yet, the shoal remains always the same; internally equal to its life as a shoal. It does not break off or wash over or expand. It stays the same in its difference.

The shoal is a gathering of life that constantly adapts *in order to remain the same*. Its shoalness is given in the fact that it is always a shoal, regardless of how the ocean disrupts it, or how *it* disrupts ocean vessels and currents.

The flux of the shoal is rooted in its uncapturability: it cannot be stopped, and most importantly it cannot be stopped *from being a shoal*.

A shoal describes a mass of material in the ocean. It also describes a group of fish.

These shoals emerge all over. Everywhere the Sea tries to reach, capturing the difference of life-forms and turning them into the salty sameness of the Sea, there are shoals resisting.

King talks at length in *The Black Shoals* about William Gerard de Brahm's 1757 'Map of the Coast of South Carolina and Parts of Georgia'. At the bottom-right corner of the map, sketched over the Atlantic Ocean, is a plantation scene in which an enslaved Black man picks indigo. This map has been stored in the Special Collections Division at Davidson College in North Carolina for many years, folded over to fit in the drawers. This folding has caused the image of the enslaved man picking indigo on the plantation to double, appearing in a ghostly, fugitive form on the other side of the map, on land.

The doubling of the fugitive slave is a coincidence of history and the practicalities of archiving, but that does not make it any less meaningful. The slave is inscribed in the Sea by the colonial cartographer, shifted off the territory of American land and cast adrift in his permanent labour, a labour that stains the hands blue through indigo. He is lost on blue, in blue, as blue.

But, over hundreds of years, this unnamed enslaved man emerges on the other side of the folded paper, marking himself on land.

The shoal is also a ghostly agency that emerges fugitively

in spaces designated precisely as the shoal's impossibility. The *territory* cannot exist as a protected, private zone unless it is a space where the shoal cannot go. But the shoal arrives.

Black shoals are forming alternative modes of escape against the Sea everywhere, but the escape route is difficult to register in the well-trained sightlines of White visuality.

* * *

The yacht is a vessel defined by being a place where fish cannot live. The yacht takes oxygen-breathing humans to the home of fish, the water that is so much heavier than air, where it is so impossible to breathe. Through the lustful yearning of the kill— and through Fishing Girls, of course—fish emerge onto yachts, exactly where they are not supposed to be.

* * *

As the Sea closes in on the Institution of Maritime Images, Etc., Idi, I keep thinking about its commanding temporality. The Sea claims itself as a beginning, which is what Tiffany King teaches us when we learn to really listen. She's been saying that since long before she could speak. She says it forever, but as the proxies of the Sea we only understand her words in relation to the beginning command.

A hundred years ago, there was a hairy cartoon villain in a forest in Germany who went by the name Meister Heidegger. From Plato to this hirsute don in a cabin, the language of European philosophy could only ever understand the beginning of life as a command. These bearded lords read the Bible and they saw a command at its beginning, and then they refused the Bible and they saw the command of the universal market, the command of empires spreading out, the command of the liberal nation-state.

London poet Caleb Femi describes this scene with precise simplicity:

A correspondent in the riot zone asked an old man about the situation & he said

this time
they demanded payment for death
& so they shook the city down for change

Unsatisfied, she asked a woman, but couldn't make out the words through her accent.

de man ded

Demanded what?

de
man
ded[109]

The language of hegemonic philosophy—the thinking of the Sea—seems like a *demand*, a resolute initiation of power, to the ears of its watery kin. But another kind of life speaks another language beyond this movement, way before it, in a time that needs no command to begin. The words always being said on the island of Blackness were *de man ded*.

The reference to the dead man, the *man ded*, returns language to its own status as language, while the pursuit of a *demand* wants to find a commanding authority that began this situation. The reporter—who could very well be Heidegger—wants to know the genesis of this scene, but the woman in the riot zone is not interested in that command. For her, the man's death is the accumulator of language, the proto-reference of life. What language turns back to is the life it speaks with.

Language for the woman in the riot zone is not an authority that disappears in death; it cannot be traced back to a genesis. Language is the life of the man, dead in a riot; her way of speaking is the sociality of her island, which is unregistrable to the news reporter.

The woman *inside* the riot zone, as the riot zone, is uninterested in how this scene can be universalized. She is interested in the internal logics of the island itself, which the reporter can only think of calling a 'riot'. When Black people are seen on an island, with a language of sociality that refers to that Black island itself, media report it as a riot.

What the American artist David Hammons knows is that the riot-woman's gesture of internal reference is precisely for the purpose of obscurity within the hegemonic language of modernity. She has another kind of language, and it is registered as darkness in the lights of the press and cameras.

For Hammons, 'outrageously magical things happen when you mess around with a symbol'.[110] In the hegemonic operation, there is a *symbol* and a *speaker*. An agent commands the symbol into being, and it takes on symbolic function in the world, or the Sea. The intention of messing around is neither to render the symbol profitable in the hipsterized aesthetics of gallery space, nor to dismiss entirely the importance of the symbol and its speaker. Instead, the purpose is to return to the antecedent condition that allowed the symbol and speaker to emerge as one single temporality, a clear line from speaker's command to symbol's endless life. Before that, beyond it, there is the enduring nothingness of time without command, of life without genesis; life as endurance. As Elena Filipovic writes about Hammons:

> Rather than trivial anecdotes of one artist's cagey behaviour, all of these accounts describe gestures that occupy the very core of Hammons's larger practice. Arguably, these gestures

are his practice. That practice is based not on the habitual art-world hope (and hype) for ultimate visibility and omnipresence, but the opposite: wilful obfuscation at the risk of obscurity. As a result, evasiveness—as an operational strategy as much as a form of ethics—hangs over his work like dust in the air.[111]

* * *

Chance the Rapper is unable to introduce anything. The logics of introduction are completely ridiculous to him. If you walk into a room where Chance stands and try to shake his hand—which I have never tried—he would just laugh and turn around. The establishment of a precise beginning, a moment from which everything coherently leads, is a farce to Chance the Rapper.

This is not only the case in Chance's music and lyrics, but in his theology, too. God never really *begins* the life of earths. Christopher Columbus's cohort retroactively wrote a narrative that established Columbus as the single moment of beginning, the expansion of the Sea as a physical force. But all of that is just narrative. In the logic of God Himself, there is no beginning. Time, divinely, is exactly and precisely meaningless.

To show his passion for the absurdity of time, Chance the Rapper refuses the refusal of giving. Because of copyright laws—the policy of 'fair use' does not apply to music—I cannot put the lyrics here, but the song I am talking about is 'Ultralight Beam' by Kanye West, the first track on his 2016 album *The Life of Pablo*. Chance the Rapper's part of the song begins at 2:34 and ends at 4:06, and I am specifically talking about the lyrics between minutes 3:38 and 3:48.

The scene is this: Chance wants to be left alone in order to sing with and for his family, without the press capturing his movements or other singers lurking on another level of the soundscape.

And then, without warning, the scene becomes biblical. The whole song is religious, it is beatific, but this is its first biblical moment. Chance is attempting to offer time and space to his disciples, who seem to be stuck in a desert. He gives them the opportunity to go wherever they want, and if they do not want to go—he is fully aware that what he can give is not what everyone wants to receive—then he will provide them with protection while they remain.

Some say they do not want to be given anything, but Chance offers them everything anyway. The ethics of sharing, for Chance, is not a binary choice of yes or no. It is the antecedent condition of being.

Sharing and its already-givenness is a material cure. Whether they want it or not, Chance will give them a coat to protect them from the rain and cold, even if they do not enter where he allows them to go.

The thing that Chance is doing is not *an offer* of sharing. It is sharing as an *ontological* condition; sharing as the basis of life, before lives even begin. Chance's sharing is not done for *me to share with you*; rather, the ethical imperative is to be endlessly aware and in the thinking practice of the already-sharedness of sharing. It's all already *ours*. Some people took it and tried to claim it as theirs. They've been doing that for hundreds of years. But it's always *ours*, beneath and beyond their violent appropriation of the undercommons, outside the logics of their property maps, everything is *ours*, and what that means is that *it's nothing*.

There is nothing to have, because there is no possession, nothing to own because there are no *things*.

Communism wants everything for everyone, but Black studies—which Chance is a part of, whether he knows it or wants it or not—has another idea, as Jared Sexton says: 'Beyond the restoration of a lost commons through redistribution (everything for everyone), there is the unimaginable loss of that all too imaginable loss itself (nothing for no one).'[112]

The logic of sharing can be stolen, but that does not mean that it was ever *possessed*. It exists way beyond the perverse violence of ownership and its sacrificial rituals of theft and revenge. This stuff—sharing as the already given ethics of music for Chance—has been stolen, even though it was never owned.

The final line of Chance's verse concerns God's reaction to this scene of giving, where giving is the condition of life. Chance describes God's statement upon making a rainbow for Noah in Genesis.

The final line of four between 3:38 and 3:48 could be in quotation marks, designating the words as spoken by God, but they could also be Chance's own riff on the absent words of God.

God made the first rainbow straight after the Flood. It cleared, Noah survived, and a rainbow came. The rainbow is a contract that creates a policy of mutually beneficial diplomacy between both interested parties: God and Israelites. God gives to Israelites the beautiful spectacle of a colourful arch in the sky; Israelites give to God the cessation of all the sin they were engaged in that caused God's rage and led to the Flood. God says to Noah, 'I do set my bow in the cloud, and it shall be for a token of a covenant between me and the earth. And it shall come to pass, when I bring a cloud over the earth, that the bow shall be seen in the cloud: and I will remember my covenant, which is between me and you and every living creature of all flesh: and the waters shall no more become a flood to destroy all flesh' (KJV, Genesis, 9:13-15).

As an official promise inscribed in the policy of polite international relations that contractually obliges the maintenance of these promises, God will never again destroy Israel and Israelites.

What God said when He made the first rainbow, then, is strangely the rainbow itself. God did not make the first rainbow and then give a speech; rather, the result of the contract between God and Israelites was the rainbow.

So the temporality of Chance's verse is confusing. It is not that God said something when He made the first rainbow; it is that God's saying something made the first rainbow. The contract was initiated by the language of international commerce and diplomatic alliances, and that resulted in the construction of an aesthetic symbol allegorically bridging the colourful division between celestial omnipotence and earthly servitude.

What God, ultimately, gave Noah's family after the Flood was not a rainbow, but rather the act of giving itself. What was offered was the knowledge of sharing, and the knowledge that sharing had always already happened anyway.

* * *

If we think about what the land means, Idi, with Tiffany Lethabo King and Katherine McKittrick, then we realize that racialization is not the process of separating particularly determined life from the land. Instead, racialization is the process of forming a deoxygenated, fluid barrier between the binaries of life's racial meaning: on one side, the land and racialized lives, and on the other, the hunters' pursuit of the trophy of Whiteness. White lives are lived on yachts in the deoxygenating Sea that expands into everything. Black lives—and by Black lives, I mean non-White lives, lives separated from the Sea—are lived in and as shoals on the oxygenated island.

The meaning of the land exists and continues to exist beyond that fluid layer of expansive movement, under the life-determining vessels of the hunters. That meaning of land is what Black life is the perseveration of. As McKittrick says:

[t]he black urban presence—black life— uncovers a mode of being human that, while often cast out from other official

118

history, is not victimized and dispossessed and wholly alien to the land; rather it redefines the terms of who and what we are vis-à-vis a cosmogony that, while painful, does not seek to inhabit a location closer to that of 'the fittest' but instead honors our mutually constitutive and relational versions of humanness.[113]

Blackness becomes a coagulation of animated matter as a shoal at the impossible border of the Sea and the territory. Blackness is neither territorial, bound entirely to land, nor oceanic, afloat in the fluid barriers between continents. Blackness is a life-form that collapses the expansion of the Sea.

We should say, Idi, that we do not mean that *all Black lives* are permanently and solely in the operation of resisting the Sea. We are not talking about a single and global action, in which all Whites are on yachts universalizing the Sea, while all Blacks (and all non-Whites are all Blacks) are forming shoals of resistance. That is not what all of this means.

What it means is that under and beyond the daily life of minor violence we all live—the police, the government, the taxi drivers, the cargo captains, the state machine, the writers—there is an *ontological* movement that we are unwillingly and unknowingly involved in. It is not that we are too stupid or distracted to know that we are involved in it. Rather, it is that we do not *necessarily have to know* we are involved in it in order to be very involved in it. It happens beyond our access to the epistemes of life; it is outside of our daily knowledge framework.

Most of our actions at the ontological level are unknown to us. Like the British writer and race theorist Jessica Perera says, the chicken shop becomes a site of ontological violence when it is used by the racializing logics of the police to criminalize and track certain (Black) people's movements.[114] It is not that every activity in a London fried chicken takeaway is politically racial and actively involved in the antiracist resistance of the

119

island against the Whitening imperialism of the (police) Sea. It is that the visual and epistemological frameworks of human life are coded already in the broad movement of a racializing ontology: humanity's collective understanding of *what life means* is inscribed in the centuries-long movements of race, gender, nationality, sexuality, ability, religion, and class, and involved already in the ontological process of making these social referents a lived reality.

Through these movements of modernity, 'the fittest' work very hard to maintain a definition of 'fitness' that means the *right to have oxygen*, which also means the right to be light, to be camouflaged in the colour of the sun instead of the colour of the undersea land. 'The fittest' achieve this by constantly depriving the shoal of oxygen, removing life from its lives.

Ben Schultz—Saviour of Fish-Men, the Second Coming of Our Saintly Rod—says that the top of a fish's body is usually dark, so that it blends in with the dark colour of the ocean when looked at from above, and the bottom of its body is usually light, so that it merges into the colour of the sky when looked at from below.[115]

What Canadian space and race scholar Katherine McKittrick magnificently adds, but without the language of islands and the Sea, is that humans are distinguished by the same arrangement. Those observed on the island of a shoal are Blackened, while those on yachts and expanding as the Sea are Whitened. These brutal ethics of observation code the meaning of life-forms everywhere.

To look inwards, however, and see oneself with an ethics of observation that cannot be accessed or understood by the outwards movement of the Sea, is a practice that breaks the visual mechanisms of the *transcendent subject*. The geographic entrapment of modernity's racializing movements, as McKittrick writes elsewhere, 'simultaneously produce[s] spatial boundaries and subject-knowledges that can subvert the perimeters of bondage'.[116]

* * *

In his rap on Kanye West's song 'Ultralight Beam', Chance the Rapper makes God's promises appear before they are made. There is no scene of arrival, no moment of expansion as territory. There is just the fact of sharedness already happening.

This reading of the rainbow scene in Genesis requires the ethics of sharing to be taken out of its surrounding Christian context. Immediately following this scene in the Book, Noah retires from his life as a survivor and sailor and opens a vineyard. He gets drunk and falls asleep naked. His son Ham sees him, while his other sons Shem and Japheth cover him with a sheet.

When Noah awakes, naked and angry from the wine and heat, he curses Ham's son Canaan to be a slave forever, and all his descendants, too.

Throughout the histories of medieval religious racism and modern transatlantic slavery, the enslavement of Black people was justified among many European Whites by referring to the curse of Ham. The justification goes that Ham was the ancestor of all enslaved Blacks, which he deserved for seeing his father naked.[117]

All of these justifications and interpretations of the narrative, however, occur much later than the writing of Genesis. Around the first millennium BCE, the writers of the Torah would not have understood God's curses as absolute and universalizing commands.

In ancient Israel, the legal codes were not laws in the sense we understand now. They had no prescriptive function. The laws were a kind of communal bond, an implicit code of social reasoning between groups of people, but judges were not bound to these laws and they were not statutory. As Irish biblical scholar John J. Collins writes in his history of the Torah,

Mesopotamian laws and the laws of Exodus 'might serve as royal propaganda, or serve various uses for scribes or priests. But they did not function as the law of the land in a prescriptive sense'.[118]

In Israel, these laws had the purpose of teaching Israelite scribes how to copy information. The purpose of the written laws was to be copied and studied by Israelites. The function of the text, that is, was the use of the text itself. Ancient Mesopotamian law was a ritual of self-creation, endlessly repeating its scene of birth by being rewritten, re-studied, onto Israelite scrolls, into Israelite minds.

This textual function of the law sets up a fundamentally Judaic tradition, which continues in Judaism today with the constant interpretation and inscription of the Talmud. The Word of God, in this practice, is not a commanding origin, an absolute moment of beginning. Rather, it is the constant operation of the constitution of the human-as-Jew. Humans turn themselves into Jews by rewriting, repeating, engaging endlessly with the movements of God.

From the beginning, 'law' was a difficult word in relation to the practices of Israelites. Within Hebrew Scripture (which is called the Tanakh in Judaism and the Old Testament in Christianity), the first five books were called 'the Law' by the time of Christ and the New Testament. These famous five books are now called the Pentateuch, or the Torah (*torah* meaning something like *law* in Hebrew). In the earliest Koine Greek translation of the Tanakh—called the Septuagint—'*torah*' is translated as '*nomos*', which refers to a specific form of Greek political law, rather than the broader and more ambivalent Hebrew use of '*torah*' among Israelites.

The Book of the Jews already begins with a problem of its own meaning, given a name that refers to the most remarkably absent part of the text: laws. In the Pentateuch—which is formed of Genesis (*Bereshit*), Exodus (*Shemot*), Leviticus

(*Vayikra*), Numbers (*Bamidbar*), and Deuteronomy (*Devarim*)—
some 40 percent of the text is made of laws, but these laws
are remarkably, famously doubtful. The laws are not followed
by anyone, even God. Every person in the narratives doubts
the law, leaves it, disbands and breaks, then returns, asks for
forgiveness and forgives. The profound complexity of the Book
and its prophets cannot be reduced to the brazen simplicity of
a commanding law.

The Torah, then, is a word that refers to the action that
does not yet happen in the Torah. Any laws that *are* given in
the Torah, as American theologian Ben Witherington III points
out, are confusing, such as the dictum against killing in the Ten
Commandments, which seems to contradict the many killings
that take place in the Torah by holy Israelites.[119] Judaism as a
model of faith and Jewishness as a historical relation to faith are
based, unstably, on doubt.

This is even more pronounced through Jews' relationship with
the Torah and the Tanakh. These Scriptures are not the holiest
texts of Judaism. It is the Talmud that has divine authority, and
the Talmud is an enormous and ongoing interpretation of the
Tanakh. The books doubt themselves, asking constant questions
of each other. As the British Jewish writer Matt Greene puts
it, 'the engine for Judaism isn't faith. It's doubt...Essentially
the Talmud is marginalia, a conversation. A beneath-the-line
comments section. What Judaism essentially amounts to is a
four-thousand-year-old argument.'[120]

The Jewish God, like His Jews, walks tentatively on His
land. He doubts the perfection of the world He made, treading
steadily over shifting desert sands. He cannot be sure that these
laws are right for this moment, or this world. It's beautiful—His
Scripture, His World, His holy Israel—but it could go wrong at
any moment. The fault-lines are written already in His status
as Hashem, as Adonai, as the doubting God of Israel. Or as the
Jewest of the Jews Woody Allen says in his stuttering doubt, 'I

never jump where there's gravity.'[121]

* * *

For the temporality of Chance the Rapper's rainbow-giving to emerge, he has to fold backwards, past his Christianity, before the New Testament Christ and his life of foundations and commands, back into the ambivalent messages of the Torah, back into the confusion of Jews.

In a lot of contemporary Jewish literature, Jewishness is defined precisely by this self-doubt. The confusing and anxious positions of never knowing whether you are really you, whether you are alive at all and whether this has all begun yet, is the condition of being Jewish, which Devorah Baum renders fittingly as Jew*ish*, and which Matt Greene, even more explicitly, calls Jew(ish).[122]

Baum sums up this self-absenting procedure of being Jewish with a typically Jewish joke:

> Two Jews, Moishe and Itzhik, are walking in the forest in the Ukraine some 150 years ago. In the distance, they see two local guys walking toward them. Moishe turns to Itzhik, panics, and says: 'Itzhik, what should we do? There's two of them, and we're all alone!'[123]

Moishe is alone because he cannot invest any faith in the idea of a singular command as himself. He has no moment of beginning, no initiation ceremony to follow. He is an ongoing sociality, together in the forest with Itzhik.

I don't know how to play the trumpet, Idi, but I'd like to toot the horns of Gabriel, only in order to celebrate the instances of *island thinking* that have emerged throughout the earths and their histories. I think the early Jews of Israel were island thinkers, turned inwards to an impossible production of themselves. They turned the walls inwards, and inside this self-writing practice they found doubt and confusion. The God of Israel is confused, never knowing whether to punish or to bless, and the people of Israel are confused, in endless exodus.

Island thinking isn't about the Zionist nationalism of contemporary Israel, which ultimately does not have the goal of turning inwards but rather of conquering, of turning the idea of insularity into an expansive principle. The result, as you know, Idi, is war, a war you fought in for 3 years.

Judaism as Mosaic Law is a limiting code. It builds walls, keeping in the Jewishness of Jews. It does not write the history of everyone or turn the lives of earth into a single World, structured on a timeframe towards the moment of becoming-Jew. Jewishness, in the Torah, is a state of doubt and insecurity; it is the process of exodus. And through that insularity, through that self-sealing of the island of Jewishness, Jews enter an internal language that escapes from the presupposed lines of global meaning. They emerge into a language that has no referent on earth. It refers only to the internal state of being Jewish, of being among Jews.

The promise of that collective Jewishness came before the creation of earth, before the expulsion from Egypt, before the revelations at Mount Sinai, before the wandering. The promise of the collective and undercommon language of Mosaic Law existed already, forever, in the vibrational sensation of being Jewish. And the rainbow, for Chance the Rapper, came before the accord between God and Israelites; the ongoing undercurrent of the promise as an internally-referential sociality was already there.

Chance the Rapper is all alone in multiple folds of truth without time. He believes that Christ is by his side, Jesus the Christian Christ of Saint Paul, but that belief rests on the necessity of forgetting that Jesus is Jewish flesh, and as such Jesus can invest no faith in *his own* singular and stable presence.

Jesus is the descendant of exile, a product of permanent desert exodus. Christ is not the *rock*, the stable presence. That rock is Saint Peter, Christ's first disciple, but even he is unsure of his rockiness. Before Christ called him a rock, a stable brother to rest a religion on, and named him Peter (from the Greek *petros*, meaning rock), he was called Simon and was a fisherman on the Sea of Galilee; before his life as rock, Simon Peter was watery. And before the telos of his Christianity, its tidy timeframe rooted in beginnings, Chance the Rapper was a Jew, in constant and confusing exodus from himself.

* * *

Either Idan the Man or Idan Hayosh the Artist—I can't tell which—says in an interview that he is not interested in political statements or national, collective guilt. He is more interested in the 'possibility of a very personal responsibility', as the interviewer puts it.[124]

In my conversations with Idan the Man about the Instagram account, he has expressed a similar concern. When I first showed him an example of what I wanted to write about his work for this book, he responded,

jesus, you're not kidding around! :D...to be honest, you don't need me :) it's already good and meaninful without the idea of collaboration, or rather, the collaboration is already happening. you revive those dead insta posts into 'a walk through H' type of thing.

He wanted to remove himself from the archaeological scene of hauling up the dead bodies, the post-war blues of inspecting every soldier, examining the bombshell damage and listing the buildings' structural weaknesses in the council archives.

For him, the scene of death was where the event ended. The

war itself is the point at which collective responsibility can go no further.

If we end up in war — either by killing fish on a yacht every day to sacrifice for the gods of Instagram, or by razing Palestine and occupying its slaughter-grounds — then collective responsibility has imploded. The possibility of imagining a single movement of society has been severed violently by the act of war itself.

Idan grew up in Ra'anana, just outside Tel Aviv, and the aesthetics of war were everywhere.

Growing up in Israel is quite a militaristic experience, in general. The overwhelming majority of the mature population goes to the army. Already in high school you're brainwashed to accept this. And also, your father did it, your grandfather did it, your siblings do it. It's the normal thing to do. You simply grow up with the aesthetics of militarism there. One out of four people carries a gun in Israel. You see guys with M16s on their backs on the street. You learn how to shoot a BB gun in high school. Today's kids have posters of Rihanna in their rooms. Kids my age had posters of airplanes, bombs, missiles, and bullets hanging on their walls. The most popular magazine back then was *Betaon Hail Hàavir*, the air force magazine, a kind of *National Geographic* of Israel, that documented the development of state-of-the-art weaponry, airplane designs, and the future of aviation.[125]

Militarism becomes a way of enveloping the elusive politics of 'defence' into an offensive and expansive outwards imperial movement. The *nation defending itself* becomes a language of expansion that claims ethical validity.

Images in this context are used to affirm the signifying function of imperial expansion. The images of guns and tanks and righteous Jews establishing their foundations are a sign that lights up the goal of conquest. The distant phenomena of magazine imagery and military bombs—and the distant audiences of magazine readers and bombed and murdered people—become connected by a semantic arch that is called 'Israel'. Israel will make the war a constant reality, because these peoples of exodus need a firm foundation for the nation-state ideology of modernity.

Nowadays, exodus doesn't have the same sexy ring as it had in the tenth century BCE; it sounded noble and holy then, but now it's just a failure of the rituals of capitalism. If you're in exodus, you're outside of the logics of accumulation. You are literally defined against the meaning of property, and property is the ultimate ontological pursuit. You lay the foundations of your life as success by building Self on Property.

Old Mosaic Jews, mates of Moses in the desert wanderings, have no such thing as external property. They themselves are their property; what they own is what they believe. Hashem is their house, and the men of the Torah are the walls of their land.

But that doesn't fit the function of imperial modernity's accumulative principles. Everything must circulate, everything must expand.

War, in this regime of aesthetics, is just normal daily practice. There is nothing special about certain kinds of murder. The murder of 'defending' soldiers or police officers is worthy of being collectively commemorated and mourned, but the murder of the 'enemy' is just the onwards movement of bureaucratic necessity. In order to render itself meaningful in the murderous ideology of modern nation-states, Israel must establish a foundation myth, a solid origin. And the foundation myths of modern nation-states always begin—like in the United States of America, like in the European Union, like in Britain, like in the French Republic, like in the People's Republic of China—with the continued dispensation of systemic and arbitrary sacrificial death.

The Muslims of Palestine are controlled and killed—as is

traditional in the formation of global nation-states—precisely for the careless imperial maintenance of the state. The 'state' only has global meaning in modernity when it constantly regulates its internal and external borders through an untraceable system of violence and brutality, through imprisonment, through war, through missiles, through austerity, through evasive voting rights.

Race theorist Arun Kundnani interestingly writes about the arbitrary nature of this state-forming brutality in relation to the murder of a Black imam in Detroit, USA. The FBI had two excuses for its murder of Imam Luqman: he was Black, and he was Muslim. So they set up a factory of stolen goods and led him to it, then detonated explosives to force him to run towards the police raid. They set a police dog onto him, which ripped apart his face, after which they shot him to death.

The killing of Imam Luqman barely registered in the news media. From one point of view, the manner of his death was hardly different from dozens of other killings of African Americans each year at the hands of militarized law enforcement agencies. From another perspective, he resembled the thousands of unnamed militants killed by drones in Pakistan, Somalia, and Yemen. Whether as an 'Islamic extremist' or as an African American, his death was a perfectly normal occurrence. If the war on terror was the stuff of high-profile debates about war, torture, and surveillance in the Bush years, under President Obama it became a matter of bureaucratic routine, undramatic and unopposed. Although Obama was elected on a wave of opposition to Bush's war on terror, he then failed to take the US in a fundamentally different direction; the administration thereby effectively neutered any remaining opposition and made permanent what had been a 'state of emergency'.[126]

In the global aesthetics of militarized life that we live inside, even here at the Institute of Maritime Images, Etc., everything is war, and war is indistinguishable from daily life for the defenders, for the Allies. For the enemy, it means death, at every corner and any moment; crushed and choked to death while buying cigarettes, shot to death while jogging, or bombed to death while trying to live, while living *as if* alive.

* * *

In *October 19, 2018*, Idi, like Patrik Alac, goes 'every day to sit by the beach'. Alac likes to observe, among many observers. Idi has a different reason: 'What i like most about the sandy landscape, is that nobody talks about credit cards there…'

The human body is a store of credit to the atmosphere. Holding captured oxygen for the purposes of removing it, turning it into another chemical. The body is always in the process of taking and giving back; in the middle of the movement of sharing. Getting out of that credit is death.

Bodies in bikinis on the beach live *as if* they were alive, *as if* they were in credit to the atmosphere.

* * *

'Ultralight Beam' itself was also late to the album *The Life of Pablo*, on which it is the first track. It arrived before the assembly of songs had been shared. As Chance recalls, he arrived at Kanye's studio to record a song for G.O.O.D. Fridays, Ye's weekly song release tradition. However, they began collaborating, began *studying*, and the constitutive, antecedent element in the album then emerged, the album having already been made and completed. 'Just the beat by itself and having the feeling of exalting and praise and worship that was not previously, it opened up the album to be everything else that it could be,'[127] as Chance says.

There is this secret, this praise before the construction of the temple, this resounding and vibrational feeling that gives away a sharedness that already comes before and beyond the sermon.

English cultural theorist Mark Fisher, talking posthumously through his friend and fellow English cultural theorist Kodwo Eshun, invested in Kanye West and Drake as 'the most important artists of the twenty-first century' precisely because of this sub-revealing operation that shares poetry's and philosophy's languages, that makes the speaker and the symbol the same thing: what is spoken is already shared, what is given is already impossible to give, already beyond the logics of ownership.

Kanye and Drake, for Fisher and Eshun, 'highlight that even if you're rich, things are terrible. Both Kanye and Drake...point out that no matter how wealthy each of them has become, there is still this deep, ineradicable sadness'. It is a 'secret sadness that lurks behind the twenty-first century's forced smile'.[128]

Fred Moten's concept of sharing centres around this perverse temporality, the throwing-to-the-end that only belatedly reveals what was already known long ago. 'Even in zones that are preserved for the protection and cultivation of normative white interests, the simple capacity for people to maintain anything like a liveable individual life...has been the function of the chorus and forced enactment and practice of sharing of women, which is to say: the *extraction of sharing*, and that's crucial. Literally, the *taking of sharing*.'[129] Sharing is shared, the Black maternal operation of already-having-given, like Chance's divine promise, but sharing is also—just as necessarily—always taken.

So 'Ultralight Beam' arrives at *The Life of Pablo*, already in an ongoing process of sharing, the beam having opened the cracks in the album long before the album was built, before any cracks were revealed. There is no moment of arrival, no origin scene, and no signifying function of these words. 'Ultralight Beam' as a sign does not refer to some other thing in the world. It has no cartographic coordinates. It refers only to itself, and to the antecedent opening it lives in and as, opening into its little hole in the undercommons that is itself.

* * *

What's the trophy? There is trophy hunting, and there are trophy wives. Is the trophy the fish or the woman holding it? Maybe it depends on their relation to the Hunter, the Photographer.

If he had lived in the age of photographic technology, celebrity toga model Aristotle would have loved a camera. He loved observing animals, expanding into their home and sitting there as territory.

For the Philosopher, animals have one of two social attitudes: gregarious, or solitary.

> Some are gregarious, some are solitary, whether they be furnished with feet or wings or be fitted for a life in the water; and some partake of both characters, the solitary and the gregarious.
>
> Gregarious creatures are, among birds, such as the pigeon, the crane, and the swan; and, by the way, no bird furnished with crooked talons is gregarious. Of creatures that live in water many kinds of fishes are gregarious, such as the so-called migrants, the tunny, the pelamys, and the bonito.
>
> Man, by the way, presents a mixture of the two characters, the gregarious and the solitary.[130]

Fish love being together, spending their days in the water with schools of kin. Aristotle notes that fish are quite singular in having only one method of transport: many land animals can walk *and* climb, or walk *and* swim, and flying animals can also walk on the land. Fish, however, have only one method of movement, and they are bound to its environment: swimming, and living, in water.

I often shamefully feel that the only environment I can survive in is contemporary capitalism and its watery ubiquity. I arrived at an airport once and all the shops were closed — the chairs were up on tables in Pret, the gates drawn over Boots, the palisades raised around duty free. I was so sad, Idi; I had nothing to buy before my plane ride. I was hungry and limp and my wallet was so heavy, I couldn't walk with it anymore. I couldn't swim, couldn't climb the slippery surfaces of the white international vortex zone.

Water is everywhere, expanding, turning everything watery.

Aristotle watches fish making love as the seasons pass, as 330BCE turns to 329, another winter endured in a breezy robe as the waters move in, as fish love.

In the neighbourhood of Lesbos, the fishes of the outer sea, or of the lagoon, bring forth their eggs or young in the lagoon; sexual union takes place in the autumn, and parturition in the spring. With fishes of the cartilaginous kind, the males and females swarm together in the autumn for the sake of sexual union; in the early summer they come swimming in, and keep apart until after parturition; the two sexes are often taken linked together in sexual union.

The force of fish love confuses him; he loses his landed footing. Are they of the outer sea or the lagoon, do they bring their eggs or their young? The sight of so much love is destabilizing for a man of rigid outer appearance, a man who arrives in disinterest, squarely geometrical, pediment-topped and lower-colonnaded.

I want to use my fish love in the lagoon to enact my disappearance from the encroaching homogeneity of the sea; I want to move away from the sameness of the water, its conquest of little patches of difference. I want to pull up a dark shawl and disappear from the view of fishermen, of mermaids and sea-gods, finding instead a gregarious school to swim about forever with.

I want to swarm in the autumn for the sake of sexual union. Open my robe of disappearance.

Of molluscs the sepia is the most cunning, and is the only species that employs its dark liquid for the sake of concealment as well as from fear: the octopus and calamary make the discharge solely from fear. These creatures never discharge the pigment in its entirety; and after a discharge the pigment accumulates again. The sepia, as has been said, often uses its colouring pigment for concealment; it shows itself in front of the pigment and then retreats back into it; it also hunts with its long tentacles not only little fishes, but oftentimes even mullets. The octopus is a stupid creature, for it will approach a man's hand if it be lowered in the water; but it is neat and thrifty in its habits: that is, it lays up stores in its nest, and, after eating up all that is eatable, it ejects the shells and sheaths of crabs and shell-fish, and the skeletons of little fishes. It seeks its prey by so changing its colour as to render it like the colour of the stones adjacent to it; it does so also when alarmed. By some the sepia is said to perform the same trick; that is, they say it can change its colour so as to make it resemble the colour of its habitat.

Some fish can turn opaque to resist the oppressive visuality of their hypervisibility. They can disappear in ink, pumping darkness out and rendering themselves rocky.

It's funny what Aristotle thinks of as stupid.

The fish approaches his hand as he dips it in the water, which Aristotle interprets as a kind of suicide drive. A fish should know better than to approach a hunter whose hand is dangling; that is a sword-hand, a slicing machine—never go

Choking on Guys and Gills

near it. But Aristotle really doesn't understand the meaning of his own hand, of the gregariousness of fish, or of the reason for that aquatic approach.

The Hunter's hand is not a hand to run away from. The Hunter can climb higher than you, run faster than you, swim deeper than you. When your mum and Canadian authorities say 'bears' they mean 'the Hunter'. 'The Hunter' means the man who is *insignificant* to look at; it means the mechanism that we see through. It means the thing that is not *seen*, but that positions the meaning of sight.

Indeed, it is stupid to run from the Photographer/Hunter. He sees you, because *seeing* is a verb that means whatever he does with you.

The octopus does not approach the Hunter's hand to get caught. The octopus knows that the Hunter is in another mode. He is not, for one thing, on a boat with his Rod, and most importantly he has left his Fishing Girls behind. There is no one to photograph with the dead fish, no one to display the kill for, so the kill is pointless. The octopus knows this pensive mode of the Man is safe, for now.

The octopus approaches the dangling-handed Hunter. The purpose of this approach is quite the opposite of suicide: it is eternity. The octopus is in search of posterity. The octopus is now in a book by the Philosopher Himself, the absolute authority on what goes into books. Aristotle wrote about that octopus because that octopus approached his hand.

Maybe it wasn't Aristotle's own hand, since the book is made of second-hand evidence collected from travellers and merchants, but it was the hand of a Hunter, just like Aristotle, and the Philosopher believes Hunters.

Aristotle is also wrong to presume that 'the only species that employs its dark liquid for the sake of concealment' is the mollusc. The same technique is used by Fishing Girls. It is this technique that allows them to evade their trade-marked skin.

Sometimes, having eluded the mark of trade on them, Fishing Girls are no longer Fishing Girls. They are animated into life and they move into motion beyond the life-form of the bikini. These kinds of animated Fishing Girls are called *female artists*.

Fishing Girls are branded in a mark that is the duplicity of non-masculine architectures: they are not honest or real like masculine classicism, as Inigo Jones says and as everyone says. They are not feminine, either. Instead, they are excessive, affected, extravagant. This is the mark of the trade in Fishing Girls: they are trade-marked by their meaning on the stage of the market. What's the value of a Fishing Girl on an Instagram photo? That sum is her trademark.

She has, however, the capacity to evade the stamp of trade. Like a mollusc, she employs dark liquid.

Not every Fishing Girl can use it, though. I don't know which ones can and which ones can't because I am a Hunter and I think anyone who approaches my swordless, cameraless hand is stupid, which I learnt from my Father, Aristotle the Younger. I think, in fact—I necessarily *must* think, otherwise I would not be a Modern Man, disaffected and disinterested—that anyone who is not topped by a triangular pediment and propped up on Doric columns, like real neoclassical Men, is stupid and excessive. There is no way I can think otherwise without unbecoming me, without disappearing in the dark liquid of my inability to see myself framed, unframed, eluded in the water everywhere.

* * *

Jennifer C. Nash, Mireille Miller-Young, Tiffany Lethabo King, M. NourbeSe Philip, Elizabeth Grosz, Grace Kyungwon Hong, Denise Ferreira da Silva, Simone Browne, Anne Boyer, Silvia Federici, Neferti X. M. Tadiar, Sianne Ngai, Jasbir K. Puar, Sylvia Wynter, Kathryn Yusoff, Dionne Brand, Nina Simone,

Katherine McKittrick—they know who can use the power of dark liquid, and how to do it. But I don't, so there's not much more I can say about that.

* * *

When English art critic John Berger becomes interested in animals, he is not interested in whether they bite his hand or not. He is millennia away from Aristotle's worries. Some say this is because Berger came second in the hotly contested Athens' Top Toga Model competitions of the fourth century BCE, just behind the Philosopher's gold position, while others say it's because Berger was part fish. His uncle—from Wapping, in east London—was a Thames trout.

Aristotle is a real outdoors man. When he talks about fish, he—or at least someone he knows—goes to Lesbos, walks to the shore, and sticks his hand in the water. By the time of Berger's life, this kind of research is called 'ancient'. When Berger writes about animals, they are in cages, or domesticated in people's houses. Everything is closed in.

It seems at first like little islands have been made on which humans and pets live together. But the domesticated house is a sign of expanding universality. It is exactly the operation of the Sea.

Aristotle's world has definable limits. He can go to the port of Athens and take a boat to Lesbos. Enslaved men will heave the oars, and Aristotle will step onto the island. Across the water, another empire expands, and he is not allowed to access it. There, cultural difference is absolute, and Athenian toga divas are not allowed in, especially after what the Philosopher's pupil Alexander the Great was up to in the east.

The limits of the twentieth-century family house are unknown. It is an expanding dream of ownership. It has very little to do with the physical placement of bricks and windows.

It is all about conquest and expansion. The house is a symbol of the possibility of ownership; the owner can own the World, if only the house could expand to a global size.

Berger, of course, already knows all of this.

> The practice of keeping animals regardless of their usefulness, the keeping, exactly, of *pets*...is a modern innovation, and, on the scale on which it exists today, is unique. It is part of that universal but personal withdrawal into the private small family unit, decorated or furnished with mementoes from the outside world, which is a distinguishing feature of consumer societies.[131]

The *universal but personal withdrawal* that defines the modern space of gathering is exactly where the practice of arbitrarily encaging animals becomes necessary. Space must be captured in order to claim an imperial reign over the family as territory. Raw materials must be captured in order to impose the authority of God-Men on the World. And animals must be put in cages to show the expansive universality of our uncaged lives.

In their domestic entrapment, these animals become proxies for the reflective expansion of Human subjectivity. The owner imposes certain traits on the animal, confirming the owner's own position. A violent dog affirms the violence of the owner. A hungry cat marks out the presence of a hungry cat-boss.

Berger notices that the reason for this projection is the desire for *universalization*. The World must become the singular possession of the Man. 'In such works [as Disney and Beatrix Potter] the pettiness of current social practices is *universalized* by being projected on to the animal kingdom.' Disney ducks await the inheritance of dead relatives. The animals live in a distant and fictional proxy of the Human World; a space, most importantly, *created by Humans* and open for Human domination.

For Berger, this has a very peculiar effect on the animals.

They all turn into fish. 'Baby owls or giraffes, the camera fixes them in a domain which, although entirely visible to the camera, will never be entered by the spectator. All animals appear like fish seen through the plate glass of an aquarium.'[132]

The fish is, in a sense, the archetype of the trapped. So silent, so unknowable, so impossible as a receptor of the subjective projections of people. No fish seems like its owner. No fish, really, even has an owner. *That's my fish...Erm, huh?*

Fish are beyond the logics of ownership with which Humans create the World as one conquerable site. Fish are the archetypes of entrapment, and yet they have a mode of being that is beyond the logics of capture. They exist, fugitively, with another language and another way of knowing.

The optics of the fish environment emphasizes this duality: it seems so accessible, the welcoming refreshment of water, the visual magnification that water imposes on the lives inside it; and yet, it is a space of death for breathing Humans, a space of silent and peaceful death.

The purpose of the zoo is to put as many species and varieties of animal as possible together, to emphasize a certain position of the Human. In the zoo, Humans convince themselves that they are the objective and omniscient observers of the World. Humans study and observe and register all existing life-forms. Since the nineteenth century, as Berger writes, zoos have claimed this cause, establishing their regime of imperial capture—which perfectly mimics the ideology of imperial capture that pervaded the nation, the museum, the navy, and the nascent racializing subjectivity of the time—by claiming to 'further knowledge and public enlightenment'.[133] The civilized Humans put animals in cages for the good of the animals.

And White British Men put Indians in the British Empire for the good of Indians, as wannabe imperial knight of the realm Rudyard Kipling celebrated:

Take up the White Man's burden—
Send forth the best ye breed—
Go send your sons to exile
To serve your captives' need
To wait in heavy harness
On fluttered folk and wild—
Your new-caught, sullen peoples,
Half devil and half child[134]

In this organized imperial space of observation, however, the *way of looking* is always wrong. Humans in the zoo must convince themselves of the benevolence of their presence. Animals *need* zoos, for some reason, and it is only through this perverse belief that Humans can continue to invest in their liberal enjoyment of life in cages.

When George Orwell's fictional British imperial police officer in Burma hears of a troubled elephant and rides his pony to it, he discovers that no one will give him any information. Burmese locals want nothing to do with this figure, convinced of his institutional benevolence in the scene. The elephant, who is smashing up the market, is a huge burden to the officer. He is desperate not to look a fool in front of the people surrounding him. He shoots the elephant and rides back to the office.[135]

In the middle of the nineteenth century, when zoos were becoming popular as a new kind of museum in the UK, Britain was the biggest empire in the world, and its most valuable colonial asset was India. In 1857, the First Indian War of Independence (known in the UK as the Indian Mutiny) began. India came so close to winning its independence that a relentless, savage regime was imposed by a new form of direct British rule. Over the next 10 years, an estimated ten million Indians were directly or indirectly killed by the British Empire.[136]

These events revealed to Britain the weakness of its rule over colonized countries. There was a heroic illusion that the mighty soldiers in their moustaches and khaki hats were boldly bringing in produce and value from overseas, but when the bloody mess and chaotic infighting of Britain's role in the Indian War of Independence was revealed, it became clear that there was nothing but a 'miniscule elite of culturally alien colonizers in a position to exercise power over an often numerically stronger "native" population'. So, as historians Harald Fisher-Tiné and Christine Whyte write, 'anxiety, fear and *angst* became part of their everyday experience'.[137]

This violent anxiety is the emotive landscape of the *wrong way of looking* that inevitably arises in the zoo. 'In principle,' Berger writes, 'each cage is a frame [a]round the animal inside it. Visitors visit the zoo to look at animals.' They move through the zoo like a gallery, observing the works. 'Yet in the zoo the view is always wrong. Like an image out of focus. One is so accustomed to this that one scarcely notices it anymore; or, rather, the apology habitually anticipates the disappointment, so that the latter is not felt.'[138]

The apology is, 'What did you expect?' It is an *animal*, alive, not some dead canvass on a wall. 'It's leading its own life. Why should this coincide with its being properly visible? Yet the reasoning of this apology is inadequate. The truth is more startling.'[139]

Once a millennia-long cohort of European White Men has established an ontological and epistemological grounding for the global imposition of the World as White Men, it is easily conceivable that all forms of life can be captured, and that their capture is for their own good. As the Californian God of Laughter Paul Beatty incomparably explains:

You'd rather be here than in Africa. The trump card all narrow-minded nativists play. If you put a cupcake to my head, of course, I'd rather be here than any place in Africa, though I hear Johannesburg ain't that bad and the surf on the Cape Verdean beaches is incredible. However, I'm not so selfish as to believe my relative happiness, including, but not limited to, twenty-four hour access to chili burgers, Blu-ray, and Aeron office chairs is worth generations of suffering. I seriously doubt that some slave ship ancestor, in those idle moments between being raped and beaten, was standing knee-deep in their own faeces rationalizing that, in the end, the generations of murder, unbearable pain and suffering, mental anguish, and rampant disease will all be worth it because someday my great-great-great-great-grandson will have Wi-Fi, no matter how slow and intermittent the signal is.[140]

But then we get to zoos and the animals won't fucking *dance for us*! This is for *their own good*, don't they realize? This is precise science here, a rigorous methodology of capture and encaging and surveying and reproducing, because who wouldn't want some underfunded biology doctoral candidate scribbling their every movement on a chart and encouraging them to penetrate the prisoner in the neighbouring cell?

Wherever you are, however you get there, as a White Man in the World you are central to the ontological operation of spacetime and map-making, while the animal in a cage is defined by being an object that is *observed*, never *seeing*.

'However you look at these animals,' Berger writes, '*you are looking at something that has been rendered absolutely marginal*; and all the concentration you can muster will never be enough to centralize it.'[141]

The title of Berger's essay is 'Why Look at Animals?' He does not directly answer the question, because the answer is already universal. The answer is the singularity of World, of the global space of the Sea in which we live. The fact of looking is itself the meaning of looking at animals. Where the glance is cast, animals appear. Whatever falls into the projective light of the racializing and expanding Human is what becomes an *animal*.

Animals are incomprehensible lives on islands, strange patches of dry earth beyond the singular visual reason of the Sea.

As Berger writes, 'it is both too easy and too evasive to use the zoo as a symbol. The zoo is a demonstration of the relations between man and animals; nothing else.'[142] But those very relations reveal the meaning of the Human way of looking. With animals put in cages and celebrated by their captors, the ravenous aggression of modern visuality is displayed with a candour that it usually hides. The elation with which we observe encaged animals in zoos provides an opening into the meaning of other visual ecstasies. The cultural spectacle involved in centuries of transatlantic slavery; the incredible popularity of online pornography, with 35 billion visits a year and 2 hours of videos uploaded every minute to just one single pornography website;[143] the traded cultural value of the feminized body on Instagram and the industry of insults, misogynist fury, and anger that accompanies it; the implicit and explicit patriarchal motives of politics, starkly revealed in uniform images of White Men controlling women's bodies.[144] These are not *the same* as zoos, but understanding and studying each of these brutal phenomena allows a point of access into all the others, and to the logic of our love of brutality.

Berger, as he always does, knows this too. He knows that driving on a road surrounded by trees is a way to understand the body, and that gardens and village restaurants are the material literature of death and beauty.

We drove up a steep dust road through the forest. Once I asked a child the way in my terrible German and the child did not understand and simply stuffed her fist into her mouth in amazement. The others laughed at me. It was raining lightly:

the trees were absolutely still. And I remember thinking as I drove round the hairpin bends that if I could define or realize the nature of the submission of the trees, I would learn something about the human body too—at least about the human body when loved. The rain ran down the trees. A leaf is so easily moved. A breath of wind is sufficient. And yet not a leaf moved.[145]

* * *

Simon was a fisherman in Bethsaida, on the eastern shores of the Sea of Galilee.

Christ the desert wanderer wandered desertly on this day, and spotted Simon, sunlight hitting the sandy robe, its salty length, on the shores of the Sea of Galilee.

Simon dropped his life as fisherman, cast into the water with his lakeside wife and holy mother, and turned away from the Sea of Galilee.

Christ waved his hand, Christly, beckoning the winds away from the Sea of Galilee.

Arrived the twain at rocky lands, high places, and Christ felt the firm footing of his place in the Christ-World, so he called the fisherman a rock, a pedestal, a Peter, far now from the Sea of Galilee.

But the denial, unmasterly, One Two Three, all the way from Simon to unpetery, through water, stone, and back to watery, sinking heavy in the Sea of Galilee.

One Two Three, they undo He, and a rock sinks in the Sea of Galilee.

* * *

A Love Song from Christ to Saint Peter, the Fisherman of Galilee

The fisherman is lapped
by pearls of salty
sea, hot foam between
the hairs; platted
ribbons of underwater weed
in the blisters of his feet.
In the rocky sea
of Galilee. Mud flaps
a tongue over pebbled
shores, the wine-red slice
of peat in the fishing sea,
Galilee is Petery. And Simon
the man-thing is standing there,
against a stone, peaty
inland fisherman, I call
him Peter, my rock.

Touch me, like Thomas
on my rocky path;
a salty island is belief.

But the sea consumes
the rock and blistered feet
sink into sand. I ran.

Unrobe these rags, untie me,
as I turn my crucifix around;
stay this side of Levantine.

The Romans came to me
while I waited, holding
up this robe, standing on
my hardened blisters.
I came here for this, Peter,

I always knew, since
the chilly evening I found
you picking bones
on the shores of Galilee.
And it ended, my
rocky Pete, when you denied
me. How could you
deny me, standing there in front of you,
my blisters hardening?
No more disciple, no Master anymore,
I am just a man, in search
of something solid. My bloody
fingers pressed together,
hair in my tears, my dress, my salty sea,
my broken rock of Galilee.

* * *

Do not deny me this, Idi: Fish are fugitives, and I don't think they're the same as the people referred to by the signs 'Woman' and 'Black', but we have been speaking about them in the same series of evenings at the Institute of Maritime Images, Etc.

Here's the thing, Idi. Fish are fugitives when they're hooked, when they are caught and photographed, joined as trophies with the trophies on the boats. Once the fish is brought into the ontological homogeneity of the Sea—where everything is and must be on a single trajectory of becoming-White and becoming-Man—then it lives with a fugitive signifying function. It carries the history of the underocean inside it, its accumulated 'bodymemory', as M. NourbeSe Philip calls it.[146] That bodymemory contains the codes of another language, a language internal to fishness that the captors on the boat cannot understand.

In this internal rupture through a different signifying

system, the fish challenges the authority of the Humans on the yacht, the Humans who claim themselves as the Universal Sea. As Moten writes in his reading of the eighteenth-century formerly-enslaved writer Olaudah Equiano, or Gustavus Vassa, 'not only [is] Equiano's humanity...on trial but...his humanity places humanity on trial'.[147]

I'm not saying the situations of fish and Equiano are the same, Idi. I'm saying that understanding and thinking about some distant things helps us understand other present things. And fish render the Human idea of the universality of the Human Sea questionable.

We begin with the null hypothesis—the assumption in the absence of evidence—that gender and race naturally exist. And then we seek the alternative hypothesis—the direction of our search for evidence—that gender and race do *not* naturally exist. Is this, I keep thinking, the right way to think?

* * *

We are hunters, Idi. What do we do with our hunterness? Tiffany Lethabo King, in another book, says, 'There is so much work that can be done on whiteness and how its coherence requires parasitism in order to survive. I think white folks have so much to do in that respect. There is this ongoing and enduring question of how does whiteness require Black death. Deal with that. What's with this obsession with us [Black people]?'[148] I quote this in everything I write, because I think it's the most important statement since solid loaves of bread saved us from those slices that fall apart when you open the pack. King tells us to study ourselves, instead of her. Maybe we should do that, Idi. Maybe we should write a book about hunters on yachts, about fish and bikinis, the Sea and the land, about our places, even though our places are very different.

Maybe we should make a mythology that resignifies the land

and the Sea. Maybe we should make a new origin narrative about boats and bikinis. I don't want to burn yachts, because my fashion sense is funded by the burning plastic industry and I don't want to lose that lucrative sponsorship. I don't want either to kill yacht hunters or bikini girls because it would be so annoying if the first time I featured in a newspaper I had this stupid haircut that I've got now. Instead I want to leave the signifiers in the world where they are, but try to change their meaning. I think, after all, that's what you do, Idi. That's your game, and your language. You use familiarity so intensely in your work and your play that the viewers' network of meaning is disturbed. Suddenly the quotidian operation of taking money out of a cash machine is ruined, because it feels so much like the ritual and sexualized slaughter of ocean animals. And the ritual catching, killing, and burning of fish seems suddenly— unpalatably, disturbingly—sexy, because it's placed right inside the frame of bikinis, and inside the frame of bikinis are the wearers of bikinis, the symbols of the militarized sex drive of this expansive and murderous modernity.

* * *

Maybe instead, Idi, we have to attend to a certain kind of knowledge that might be called fish-knowhow, or the aquatic epistemes of gill-life, or fish-dance, or for-the-love-of-fish.

There's another problem, though. The precise figures and data are not really the problem, as we have been discussing for so long here in our maritime institute. The propositions we put forward are not the problem. The problems are the language that presupposes the possibility of putting forward propositions, and the fact that we two here—these two Men— can pass language back and forth between us, wrapped into images of dead fish and women in bikinis.

We can love fish, for sure. We can burn down the yachts

and lock up the men who captain them. We can think of grand epistemologies that release the trophies from their trophy-duty. But not much changes, in the end. We are using the same coordinates of social signifying for our love-machine; we project our love as expanding terrain, conquering the unloved space of the ocean, the fishy undersea, and the bikinis on their Fishing Girls.

The problem of love is the endlessness of expanding terrain. It grows and seeps into everything. It *becomes* everything, all the same.

When it expands, it is *terrain*, marked in the bullshit politics of nation-states. When it stays, looking inwards, self-focused — so self-focused that it reveals the absence of any singular self inside it — it is *land*.

So Fred Moten, talking to American contemporary artist Sondra Perry, says, 'We gotta get us some land. Land, preferably, that nobody else wants to live on.' Moten and Perry need a space, just a place to be, to settle the shoal against the constant fissure and disfigurement of the Sea. Just some way to be, in a place, on the land, without the violence of rental obligations and the reproductive logics of capital's unending global circulation. This land will be a place where others can be, an open shoal, a school of stillness where study stays exactly where it is, tunnelling into the undercommons, not playing the game of movement and expansion that the Sea attempts to impose. 'And if there's anybody there [on that land] already, then, you know, we have to attend to them, and ask their permission; see what they need, and see if it's OK for us to be there...Because if you bring your weirdness, you know, you gotta get permission.' That's permission to care for and with the life that exists already on the land; permission to cohabit, to live together, on a patch of land. In that permissive space, where agreement is formed for thinking together in the shoal of the undercommons, the reach of the Sea becomes impossible. Indeed, it's the incessant reach of the Sea that makes this little patch of land so wonderful.

> It seems harder and harder every day to live with the contradictions that exist as a function of having to enter into these institutions that have been ostensibly set aside for that thing that you love [i.e. *study*], recognizing that these institutions are decaying, or festering cesspools in all kinds of ways, whether it's the ubiquity of harassment and predatory sexual behaviour in art schools or in universities, or the university as glorified real estate company; is there some place we can go to do what we do, or what we want to do?[149]

For Moten, *modernity* itself—which is also known as coloniality, the mode of colonial being that is modernity—is a problem of terrain. He says, riffing heavily on the work of his hero Denise Ferreira da Silva,

> What if the problem isn't coloniality as an episteme? What if the problem is that coloniality is always already given in the very idea of the episteme? What if coloniality is the age, or the locale, or more precisely, the spacetime, of the episteme?[150]

The process of making this imperial terrain of men on yachts photographing Fishing Girls can never really be achieved by returning fish to the Sea. The return is always impossible; the state returned to is already lost in the fact of it having to be returned to.

Moten instead looks for a little piece of land where people can gather and study together, not necessarily *against* the Sea, but certainly without and away from the Sea; a place where people can practise being alive on a piece of land where no one is extracting for the purpose of expansion, where the life on land is itself the practice of landed life-forms.

Instead of returning fish to the Sea, what can be done is the reconfiguration of the fish's meaning to itself. But we should not presume that the fish need us to do this for them. They've already been doing it for thousands of years, ever since they pinched Aristotle's hand and he called them stupid.

For our purposes, Idi, I think we have to try and undo the semantics of our own constituting geographies. Our subjectivity is already a cohering internal geography marking lands of greater and lesser value within the bodies of earth, and it is that terrain that we can shift, destabilizing its horrible comfort on yachted water.

Our bodies are cartographies of violence. Our skin is scratched with the marks of our expanding history, with the stain of outwards movement and the project of homogenization. Everything becomes the same at the border of our bodies; we are washed into the Sea or the shoal.

But the closed space of inwards study is where the Sea cannot reach, where the fish can speak fishily, with a different, incoherent constitution of the self; a practice of prayer, of dance, of study without the institution, on a little piece of land that we can call our own.

Endnotes

1   Elizabeth Grosz, *Architecture from the Outside: Essays on Virtual and Real Space* (Cambridge, MA: The MIT Press, 2001).

2   Grosz, *Architecture from the Outside*, 35.

3   Aristotle, trans. David Ross, *The Nicomachean Ethics* (Oxford: Oxford University Press, 1980), 13-14 (I, 7: 1097b25-1098a15).

4   Aristotle, *The Nicomachean Ethics*, 13-14.

5   Grace Kyungwon Hong, *Death beyond Disavowal: The Impossible Politics of Difference* (Minneapolis: University of Minnesota Press, 2015), 68.

6   Hong, *Death beyond Disavowal*, 70-72.

7   Silvia Federici, *Wages against Housework* (Bristol: Falling Wall Press, 1975).

8   See: Sylvia Wynter, '1492: A New World View', 5-57, in Vera Lawrence Hyatt and Rex M. Nettleford (eds.), *Race, Discourse and the Origin of the Americas: A New World View* (Washington, DC: Smithsonian Books, 1994).

9   Simone Brown, *Dark Matters: On the Surveillance of Blackness* (Durham, NC: Duke University Press, 2015), 39.

10 Grosz, *Architecture from the Outside*, 46.

11 Simone Weil, *An Anthology*, ed. Siân Miles (London: Penguin Classics, 2005), 9.

12 Anne Boyer, 'The Girls' City', 20-22, in Fred Wah and Amy De'Ath (eds.), *Toward. Some. Air: Remarks on Poetics* (Banff, Alberta: Banff Centre Press, 2015), 21.

13 M. NourbeSe Philip, *Blank: Essays and Interviews* (Toronto: BookThug Press, 2017), 106 of Apple Books edition.

14 Philip, *Blank*, 84.

15 Tariq Jazeel, 'Spatializing Difference Beyond Cosmopolitanism: Rethinking Planetary Futures', *Theory,*

Culture and Society, Vol. 28, Issue 5, 75-97 (2011), 85.

16   Tiffany Lethabo King, *The Black Shoals: Offshore Formations of Black and Native Studies* (Durham, NC: Duke University Press, 2019), 118.

17   Robert Lowell, *Life Studies* (London: Faber and Faber, 2001 [1959]).

18   Pier Vittorio Aureli, *The Possibility of an Absolute Architecture* (Cambridge, MA: The MIT Press, 2011).

19   Aureli, *Absolute Architecture*, xi.

20   Neferti X. M. Tadiar, 'City Everywhere', *Theory, Culture & Society*, Vol. 33, Issue 7-8, 57-83 (2016), 60. Emphasis in original.

21   Tadiar, 'City Everywhere', 61.

22   Tadiar, 'City Everywhere', 62. Emphasis in original.

23   Aureli, *Absolute Architecture*, xi-xii.

24   Fred Moten, *Stolen Life* (Durham, NC: Duke University Press, 2018), 158.

25   Moten, *Stolen Life*, 158.

26   W. Chan Kim and Renée Mauborgne, *Blue Ocean Strategy, Expanded Edition: How to Create Uncontested Market Space and Make the Competition Irrelevant* (Cambridge, MA: Harvard Business Review Press, 2015), 8 of Apple Books edition.

27   Kim and Mauborgne, *Blue Ocean Strategy*, 9.

28   Kim and Mauborgne, *Blue Ocean Strategy*, 34.

29   Kim and Mauborgne, *Blue Ocean Strategy*, 58. Emphasis in original.

30   David Abulafia, *The Boundless Sea: A Human History of the Oceans* (Oxford: Oxford University Press, 2019).

31   Admiral James Stavridis, *Sea Power: The History and Geopolitics of the World's Oceans* (London: Penguin, 2017).

32   Emily Ratajkowski, 'Baby Woman', *Lenny* (2016) <https://www.lennyletter.com/story/emily-ratajkowski-baby-woman>.

33   Grosz, *Architecture from the* Outside, 32.

34   Howard Jacobson, 'Howard Jacobson on Comedy and the Finkler Question', *Schwartz Media* (2013) <https://www.youtube.com/watch?v=CYoqciWkzBk>.

35   Will Self, 'The novel is dead (this time it's for real)', *The Guardian* (2014) < https://www.theguardian.com/books/2014/may/02/will-self-novel-dead-literary-fiction>.

36   Lionel Shriver, in Rachel Cooke, 'Lionel Shriver: "Few writers are willing to put themselves on the line for free speech"', *The Guardian* (2018) < https://www.theguardian.com/books/2018/apr/14/lionel-shriver-property-metoo-cultural-appropriation>.

37   Harold Bloom, *The Anxiety of Influence: A Theory of Poetry* (Oxford: Oxford University Press, 1997), xvi.

38   Patrik Alac, *Bikini Story* (New York: Parkstone Press International, 2012), 123.

39   Aureli, *The Possibility of an Absolute Architecture.*

40   Pier Vittorio Aureli and Martino Tattara, 'STOP CITY', *Perspecta*, Vol. 43, 47-53 (2010), 53.

41   Emma Watson, in Jessica Chastain, 'Emma Watson', *Interview Magazine* (2017) < https://www.interviewmagazine.com/film/emma-watson-1>.

42   No author, *Art Mag*, 'No Escape: Idan Hayosh's Suggestive Threat Scenarios' (2013) <https://db-artmag.com/en/79/feature/no-escape-idan-hayoshs-suggestive-threat-scenarios/>.

43   Sianne Ngai, *Ugly Feelings* (Cambridge, Mass.: Harvard University Press, 2005), 94-95.

44   Dionne Brand, *A Map to the Door of No Return: Notes to Belonging* (Toronto: Vintage Canada, 2001), 54 of Apple Books edition.

45   Stephen Pokornowski, 'Vulnerable Life: Zombies, Global Biopolitics, and the Reproduction of Structural Violence', *Humanities*, Vol. 5, No. 71 (2016), 5.

46   Ngai, *Ugly Feelings*, 95.

47   Jasbir K. Puar, 'Bodies with New Organs: Becoming Trans, Becoming Disabled', *Social Text*, Vol. 33, No. 3, 45-73 (2015), 46.

48   Puar, 'Bodies with New Organs', 52.

49   Puar, 'Bodies with New Organs', 47.

50   Puar, 'Bodies with New Organs', 53.

51   Paul B. Preciado, *An Apartment on Uranus*, trans. Charlotte Mandell (London: Fitzcarraldo Editions, 2019), 183-185.

52   Mireille Miller-Young, *A Taste for Brown Sugar: Black Women in Pornography* (London: Duke University Press, 2014), 33.

53   Miller-Young, *A Taste for Brown Sugar*, 7-8.

54   Kathryn Yusoff, 'White Utopia / Black Inferno: Life on a Geological Spike', *e-flux*, #97 (2019) < https://www.e-flux.com/journal/97/252226/white-utopia-black-inferno-life-on-a-geologic-spike/>.

55   King, *The Black Shoals*, 123.

56   Lena Waithe, in Trevor Noah, 'Making Urgent Art About the Black Experience with "Queen & Slim"', *The Daily Show* (2019) < https://www.youtube.com/watch?v=5r6ZbBdGDu4>.

57   Melina Matsoukas, *Queen & Slim* (USA: 3 Black Dot, 2019).

58   Jared Sexton, 'The Social Life of Social Death: On Afro-Pessimism and Black Optimism', *InTensions Journal*, Issue 5, 1-47 (2011), 5.

59   Sexton, 'Social Life', 6-7.

60   Fred Moten, 'The Case of Blackness', *Criticism*, Vol. 50, No. 2, 177-218 (2008), 180.

61   Moten, 'The Case of Blackness', 180.

62   Frantz Fanon, *Black Skin, White Masks*, trans. Charles Lam Markmann (London: Picador, 1970 [1967]), 77.

63   Moten, 'The Case of Blackness', 179.

64   Moten, 'The Case of Blackness', 187.

65   David Marriott, 'Corpsing; or, The Matter of Black Life', *Cultural Critique*, Vol. 94, 32-64 (2016), 32-34.

66 Marriott, 'Corpsing', 34.

67 Marriott, 'Corpsing', 35.

68 Marriott, 'Corpsing', 36.

69 Cedric Robinson, *Black Marxism: The Making of the Black Radical Tradition* (Chapel Hill, NC: The University of North Carolina Press, 2000 [1983]), 171.

70 Nina Simone, 'Go Limp' (Live at Carnegie Hall, New York, 1964), track 6, *Nina Simone in Concert* (Amsterdam: Philips, 1964).

71 Jennifer C. Nash, *The Black Body in Ecstasy: Reading Race, Reading Pornography* (Durham, NC: Duke University Press, 2014), 29.

72 Nash, *The Black Body in Ecstasy*, 30. Emphasis in original.

73 Moten, *Stolen Life*, 10.

74 Moten, *Stolen Life*, 108.

75 Nash, *The Black Body in Ecstasy*, 41.

76 For a specific account of this, see: C. Riley Snorton, *Black on Both Sides: A Racial History of Trans Identity* (Minneapolis, MN: University of Minnesota Press, 2017), esp. chapter one, 17-53.

77 Nash, *The Black Body in Ecstasy*, 41.

78 Nash, *The Black Body in Ecstasy*, 47.

79 Jun'ichirō Tanizaki, *In Praise of Shadows*, trans. Thomas J. Harper and Edward G. Seidensticker (London: Vintage, 2001), 21.

80 Tanizaki, *In Praise of Shadows*, 20.

81 Later in the same essay, Tanizaki relates this different aesthetics to race and gender, at which point his writing becomes bigoted and reactionary, but while focusing solely on quotidian objects, I think Tanizaki more genuinely praises shadows.

82 Tanizaki, *In Praise of Shadows*, 13-14.

83 From <https://www.bikiniatoll.com/>.

84 Jack Niedenthal, 'A Short History of the People of Bikini

Atoll' (no date) <https://www.bikiniatoll.com/>.

85 Craig Santos Perez, 'Guam and Archipelagic American Studies', 97-112, in Brian Russell Roberts and Michelle Ann Stephens (eds.), *Archipelagic American Studies* (Durham, NC: Duke University Press, 2017), 105.

86 Santos Perez, 'Guam and Archipelagic American Studies', 106.

87 Melvin Won Pat-Borja, 'No Deal' (no date), in Santos Perez, 'Guam and Archipelagic American Studies', 106-107.

88 Won Pat-Borja, 'No Deal'.

89 Judith Schalansky, *Pocket Atlas of Remote Islands: Fifty Islands I have not visited and never will* (London: Penguin, 2012), 142-145.

90 < https://www.bikiniatoll.com/>.

91 Kathy Jetñil-Kijiner and Aka Niviâna, 'It's Time to Rise' (no date) < https://www.kathyjetnilkijiner.com/>.

92 Jetñil-Kijiner and Niviâna, 'It's Time to Rise'.

93 Won Pat-Borja, 'No Deal'.

94 Sean, 'Celebrating Female Anglers', FishingBooker blog (2019) <https://fishingbooker.com/blog/celebrating-female-anglers-womens-day-2019/>.

95 Moten, *Stolen Life*, 16.

96 Cited in Michael Levey, *A History of Western Art* (London: Book Club Associates, 1973 [1968]), 212.

97 Levey, *A History of Western Art*, 219.

98 Levey, *A History of Western Art*, 223.

99 Giorgio Vasari, *Lives of the Artists*, trans. George Bull (Harmondsworth: Penguin, 1965), 133.

100 Ben Schultz, *Ben Schultz's Field Guide to Saltwater Fish* (Hoboken, NJ: Wiley, 2003), 5.

101 *Urban Dictionary*, 'fishing' (2010) <https://www.urbandictionary.com/define.php?term=fishing>.

102 Nash, *The Black Body in Ecstasy*, 24.

103 Nash, *The Black Body in Ecstasy*, 58.

104 Alac, *Bikini Story*, 8.

105 Alac, *Bikini Story*, 8-12.

106 Sylvia Wynter and Katherine McKittrick, 'Unparalleled Catastrophe for Our Species? Or, to Give Humanness a Different Future: Conversations', 9-89, in Katherine McKittrick (ed.), *Sylvia Wynter: On Being Human as Praxis* (Durham, NC: Duke University Press, 2015), 10.

107 King, *The Black Shoals*, 115.

108 King, *The Black Shoals*, 116.

109 Caleb Femi, '*Schrödinger's Black*', *Poor* (London: Penguin, 2020), 30-31.

110 David Hammons, in Elena Filipovic, *David Hammons: Blizaard Ball Sale* (London: Afterall Books, 2017), 40.

111 Filipovic, *David Hammons*, 33.

112 Jared Sexton, 'The *Vel* of Slavery: Tracking the Figure of the Unsovereign', 94-117, in Tiffany Lethabo King, Jenell Navarro, Andrea Smith (eds), *Otherwise Worlds: Against Settler Colonialism and Anti-Blackness* (Durham, NC: Duke University Press, 2020), 109.

113 Katherine McKittrick, cited in King, *The Black Shoals*, 111.

114 Jessica Perera, *The London Clearances: Race, Housing and Policing* (London: The Institute of Race Relations, 2019), 27. < https://irr.org.uk/app/uploads/2019/02/The-London-Clearances-Race-Housing-and-Policing.pdf>.

115 Schultz, *Ben Schultz's Field Guide*, 5-6.

116 Katherine McKittrick, *Demonic Grounds: Black Women and the Cartographies of Struggle* (Minneapolis, MN: The University of Minnesota Press, 2006), 49.

117 Ibram X. Kendi, *Stamped from the Beginning: The Definitive History of Racist Ideas in America* (New York: Nation Books, 2016), 21.

118 John J. Collins, *The Invention of Judaism: Torah and Jewish Identity from Deuteronomy to Paul* (Oakland, CA: University of California Press, 2017), 25.

119 Ben Witherington III, *Torah Old and New: Exegesis, Intertextuality, and Hermeneutics* (Minneapolis, MN: Fortress Press, 2018), xxii.

120 Matt Greene, *Jew(ish): A primer, a memoir, a manual, a plea* (Seattle, WA: Little A, 2020), 16.

121 Woody Allen, *Crisis in Six Scenes*, Season 1, Episode 5, Amazon Prime Video (30 September 2016).

122 Greene, *Jew(ish)*.

123 Baum, *Feeling Jewish*, 247 of Apple Books edition.

124 *Art Mag*, 'No Escape'.

125 *Art Mag*, 'No Escape'.

126 Arun Kundnani, *The Muslims Are Coming! Islamophobia, Extremism, and the Domestic War on Terror* (London: Verso, 2014), 12 on Apple Books.

127 Chance the Rapper, in Joyce, 'Chance The Rapper Reveals "Ultralight Beam" Was For G.O.O.D. Fridays', *Complex* (2016) < https://www.complex.com/pigeons-and-planes/2016/11/chance-the-rapper-bbc-1-radio-interview>.

128 Kodwo Eshun, 'Mark Fisher Memorial Lecture', Goldsmiths, University of London (2018) <https://repeaterbooks.com/watch-kodwo-eshuns-inaugural-mark-fisher-memorial-lecture/>.

129 Fred Moten, '"Wildcat the Totality": Fred Moten and Stefano Harney Revisit *The Undercommons* in a Time of Pandemic and Rebellion', *Millennials Are Killing Capitalism* podcast (2020) <https://millennialsarekillingcapitalism.libsyn.com/>, minutes 36-41.

130 Aristotle, *The History of Animals*, trans. D'Arcy Wentworth Thompson (no date) < http://classics.mit.edu/Aristotle/history_anim.mb.txt>.

131 John Berger, *Why Look at Animals?* (London: Penguin, 2009), 24.

132 Berger, *Why Look at Animals?* 26.

133 Berger, *Why Look at Animals?* 31.

134 Rudyard Kipling, 'The White Man's Burden: The United States & the Philippine Islands' (1899) <http://www.kiplingsociety.co.uk/poems_burden.htm>.

135 George Orwell, 'Shooting an Elephant' (1936) < http://www.orwell.ru/library/articles/elephant/english/e_eleph>.

136 Randeep Ramesh, 'India's secret history: "A holocaust, one where millions disappeared..."' in *The Guardian* (2007) < https://www.theguardian.com/world/2007/aug/24/india.randeepramesh>.

137 Harald Fisher-Tiné and Christine Whyte, 'Introduction', in Harald Fisher-Tiné (ed.), *Anxieties, Fear and Panic in Colonial Settings: Empires on the Verge of a Nervous Breakdown* (New York: Springer, 2017), 1-2. Emphasis in original.

138 Berger, *Why Look at Animals?* 33.

139 Berger, *Why Look at Animals?* 34.

140 Paul Beatty, *The Sellout* (London: Oneworld Publications, 2016), 219.

141 Berger, *Why Look at Animals?* 34. Emphasis in original.

142 Berger, *Why Look at Animals?* 36.

143 No author, 'Pornography', *Enough Is Enough* (2019) <https://enough.org/stats_porn_industry>.

144 Jacqueline Rose, 'Damage: The silent forms of violence against women', in *The Guardian* (2021) < https://www.theguardian.com/news/2021/mar/30/damage-the-silent-forms-of-violence-against-women>.

145 Berger, *Why Look at Animals?* 89.

146 In McKittrick, *Demonic Grounds*, 49.

147 Moten, *Stolen Life*, 53.

148 Tiffany Lethabo King and Frank B. Wilderson III, 'Staying Ready for Black Study', 52-73, in King, Navarro, and Smith, *Otherwise Worlds*, 56.

149 Fred Moten and Sondra Perry, 'Fred Moten in conversation with Sondra Perry', *Frieze* Podcast (2018) <http://podcasts.frieze.com/?name=2018-12-10_fny18_talks_audio_fred_

moten_and_sondra_perry.mp3>, 25-30.

150 Fred Moten, *'come on, get it!* with Thom Donovan, Malik Gaines, Ethan Philbrick, Wikipedia and the Online Etymology Dictionary', *The New Inquiry* (2018) < https://thenewinquiry.com/come_on_get_it/>.

Idan Hayosh's Institute of Maritime Images, Etc.

October 30, 2018

i went to a store and stole some clothes, i was walking out very
slowly, so someone could catch me and we could talk about it
and i could say my name out loud. but nobody came
hashtag=tomatoes_have_feelings_too

November 2, 2018
they said i could not become a citizen where i live, so i built
my own country. in the west side of my bathroom. but i don't
think i wanna be president, cause then i'll have to talk to
people...
hashtag=when_you_go_away_your_dna_still_remains

March 20, 2019

last month my wife left me cause i sent the wrong emoji to her
telephone. the problem is that my hands and fingers are real
big and bulky, and hardened from years of physical work, so i
can't swipe or hit the right point on the phone screen, or that i
hit three things at the same time, and two when i really focus,
but never one. thus the wrong emoji...my wife said that it's
2019 and now most boyz got soft hands cause they use creams,
and they can write fast on their telephones, and i can't, so i
don't fit the times. she also said that us being together is not
working for her. because she wants to live with a modern man.
the kind that hits the right emoji. after she left i went outside,
took my axe and started chopping wood, cause it makes me
calm...

hashtag=knock_on_the_door_and_run_away_giggling

April 16, 2019

my auto-correct had told me once that i can't write something
like 'iiusgzdfaebgfvkejbhsgvkjlvnoesh', cause it does not fit
our society and that auto-correction is the standard in every
writing program and machine of our times, cause folks wanna
make only correct things nowadays. plus, if everyone could
use their imagination and whims of playfulness and easily
write words like 'iiusgzdfaebgfvkejbhsgvkjlvnoesh' just for
kicks, and insist they should have the option of doing that,
then the auto-correct people would gradually be challenged,
and eventually lose their job, and the last thing i want is to
cause trouble to the world. so i stopped this imagination stuff.
hashtag=I_am_google-earthing_my_street_today_cause_i_am_
too_lazy_to_go_downstairs

May 9, 2019

my girlfriend left me cause my telephone skills screwed things
up. i wanted to send this emoji with red hearts kisses coming
out of the mouth, but i'm colour blind so i mistakenly chose
this green vomit mouth emoji. so she left. i know it's 2019, and
these days one emoji is worth a thousand words, but if you
send the wrong thing, then it's a thousand wrong words, and
it's not fair. so i'm writing whomever runs the internet that it's
not fair.

hashtag=there's_more_than_one_way_to_use_your_nose

166

July 17, 2019

my girlfriend left me cause i am not good at some stuff. the thing is, that for her birthday present i took a seven-month course in origami and other paper folding techniques, and in this course they said the most basic origami animal, the swan, is the thing we will both start with and also end with, because it's not about the variety of paper animals that one can make, but rather in the quality and precision of making it. so i made her a swan. but she got angry and told me she's very disappointed in me, that using physical paper as a gift just makes the wood cutting industry thrive, and in turn, it makes the rainforests in America decline and deforest, so i'm basically a criminal. she also said that paper deteriorates in time, and that heart emojis on the phone stay forever, and that by giving her a gift that would eventually wither away and that makes our planet less green, i unconsciously project an ending to our relationship, as much as the world's. and that's something she would not stand. so she left. after that, i called the origami teacher and asked her out for a date, but she told me i should write her a letter first. with paper.
hashtag=have_fun_cause_the_alternative_is_no_fun

August 5, 2019

i first saw you when the iPhone 1 came out. we were young and you wore golden shoes that matched your phone case. it was only in the era of the iPhone 3GS that i gathered the nerve to ask you out. you said no, but that it's not cause i ain't cute, just because you had a boyfriend. when the iPhone 4 broke the market, i had heard you broke up with that dude, but we didn't see each other till 4 months later, when the iPhone 4S was released. we dated throughout the times of iPhone 5, but it was only after the iPhone 5C (and the iPhone 5S of course) came out that i knew i loved you. when i told you, you responded coldly, till you reciprocated my love when the iPhone 6 (and iPhone 6 Plus) arrived. i was not the same person though, and we separated, and then broke up, and spent the epochs of iPhone 6S, iPhone SE, iPhone 7, iPhone 7 Plus, iPhone 8, and iPhone 8 Plus away from one another. but on the day the iPhone X swept the world, i could not hold it any longer and stood under your windowsill, and told you i wanted you back. you said you'd think about it. you also said your phone is out of battery, and asked if i had a charger. hashtag=go_but_come_back_after_ok?

August 14, 2019
my girlfriend left me cause i voted for the wrong party in the
last election. the point is that our country has a lot of rain and
precipitation throughout the year, and my dyslexia is really
funny sometimes, and it makes me switch letters in words
and confuse the layout in paragraphs, so i confused the word
'irrigation' with 'immigration', and these politicians were very
strong against irrigation and they were shouting it all over
the media that over-irrigation puts a weight on expenses, and
economy for local citizens, and so i agreed, and thought, why
not stop this silly irrigation thing, when we're so blessed and
got so much of it already coming from the sky...so i voted for
them. and told my girlfriend. and so she left.
hashtag=heart_emojis_stay_forever_but_real_hearts_stop_
at_a_certain_point

February 19, 2020
i stopped taking showers cause i can't bring my telephone
inside cause it's too wet and steamy there. i had recently
bought a super expensive shower proof phone cover, but my
fingers got soft and wrinkly real quick under the hot water and
steam, so i couldn't swipe or zoom. so it's not compatible. and
the idea of standing in that shower one more time for a few
minutes confronted with only boring reality and nothing else,
makes me feel trapped without an exit plan.
hashtag=there's_an_app_that_allows_you_to_fake_your_
voice_so_it_would_actually_sound_like_you_are_happy

October 22, 2020

so the bank folks told me that my bank account is empty cause i wasted all the money i had on real dumb things. so i told them to refill it back with money. so they told me it does not work that way. so i asked them why does it not work that way. so they told me that they don't do that, and that i gotta get money myself, and then refill my account. so i asked them how to do that. so they told me i gotta get a job. so i laughed and hung up the phone.
hashtag=find_a_venimous_snake_and_get_bitten_one_last_time_cause_2021_is_cure_year

February 9, 2021

i woke up the other day and thought i should surprise myself
with a spontaneous act of self empowerment, so i bought
a coconut flavoured white chocolate bar at the cheap store
around the corner and ate it, and it tasted good, and when the
old lady who passed the corner asked me why the hell am i
smiling in the middle of a crazy pandemic that kills everybody
around us, i said that i am smiling cause the coconut flavoured
white chocolate i am eating tastes good. and i think my
telephone somehow heard this, and started plotting. so for 6
weeks, every goddamned day, i was getting coconut themed
ads on my phone. and it wasn't about coconut white chocolate
anymore, but also about coconut flavoured deodorants, and
coconut flavoured car window cleaner sprays, and coconut cat
collars, and coconut condoms, and even plain coconuts, and
all that jive. so one day i got fed up and bought all the coconut
things that my phone wanted me to buy. i spent a third of all
the money i had in the bank, and it worked, and now i don't
get any coconut ads no more.
hashtag=take_me_to_the_laundromat_and_show_me_that_
everything_is_a_cycle

February 15, 2021
my PlayStation broke down from overheating and stuff. so i
bought a play-station. a play-station (not to be confused with
PlayStation) is a wooden box with different doors and drawers
and four buttons, and so the drawers and door cabinets are
all empty, and the idea is that you gotta find content to put in
them, and the four buttons don't do anything when you push
em, so you gotta invent ideas of what they could do and when
you push em, pretend that something happens. so my play-
station's set up like this: i had put candy in all the drawers,
i had put candy in all the door cabinets, and out of the four
buttons, three of them have the same imaginary function of
making my girlfriend instantly stop being angry at me and
make peace. i did three buttons of that function just in case
some of them don't work, and she's still angry. the last button
has the imaginary function of making me instantly stop being
angry at my girlfriend and make peace. and i did not use that
one yet, but hey, who knows, today is a new day.
hashtag=use_your_muse

Author Biography

Elliot C. Mason is a writer, poet, and PhD candidate at Uppsala University. His doctoral research is focused on the spatiality of contemporary Black American poetry. He is the author of two collections of poetry and two nonfiction books. *Building Black: Towards Antiracist Architecture*, which was shortlisted for the Fitzcarraldo Essay Prize 2020, is published by Punctum Books. His essays and poems have appeared widely in publications including *Tribune, 3:AM, SPAM, Magma, Radical Housing Journal* and *The Journal of Italian Philosophy*. He is also the author of three plays, all political comedies, which have been performed at many London theatres.

Before beginning his PhD, he studied at Goldsmiths College, the University of Malta, Brighton University, and King's College London, and worked in the education sector.

Having lived in London for 10 years, in 2021 he moved to Sweden with his partner, Eugenia Lapteva.

Previous Titles

Building Black: Towards Antiracist Architecture, **Punctum Books (late 2021)**
Building Black is a radical proposition for a new concept of antiracist architectural thinking. The agency of urban forms in the construction of race as a social referent has rarely been questioned. In this book, through sustained criticisms of Kantian subjectivity and the emergence of architectural perspective, poet and cultural theorist Elliot C. Mason develops a model for archipelagic urban thinking, resisting the universalizing function of architecture's racializing impulse. Through multiform critiques of architectural theory and Western philosophy, and close engagements with Black studies and Indigenous thinking, Mason criticizes the writing subject as a collaborator in the racialization of urban cartography. In this book, Mason turns inwards, opening the impossibility of the writer's position in architecture and philosophy, and setting up a new mode of self-critical architectural writing. *Building Black* is an innovative contribution to Black and spatial studies, as well as a method of writing about space and race.

Materials for Building a City, **Marble Books (2021)**
This pamphlet takes the reader through a range of London scenes. The canal demands to know where a missing body was taken, looking through blue lights at the city's embarrassment. The flash of Tinder messages is the only guide in a chicken shop with the lights off. In Victoria Park, woodland animals stage a communist protest, but the sunbathers are distracted by another sound. *Materials for Building a City* is a powerful and disturbing portrait of life in contemporary London.

City Embers, Death of Workers Whilst Building Skyscrapers Press (2020)

City Embers is a collection of poetry and essays about housing and homelessness in London. Mason wrote the book while working at Highway House homeless shelter in Tottenham, north London, and each of its texts focuses on the life of a resident, parted by poetic reflections on the impossibility of being housed in the capital. The book is printed in two layers, with one side forming a criticism of the other, setting up an internal argument that makes domestic comfort a struggle even within the pages themselves.

Note to Reader

For any publicity or event requests, or for general feedback, write to me directly at elliotcmason@pennydropscollective.org

If you would like to read more of my work, find a full list of publications, lots of links, and other materials on my website: https://pennydropscollective.org/

Follow me on social media for regular updates. Twitter: @ ElliotCMason. Instagram: @PennyDropsCollective.

References

No author (2019), 'Pornography', *Enough Is Enough* < https://enough.org/stats_porn_industry>.

No author (2013), *Art Mag*, 'No Escape: Idan Hayosh's Suggestive Threat Scenarios' <https://db-artmag.com/en/79/feature/no-escape-idan-hayoshs-suggestive-threat-scenarios/>.

Abulafia, David (2019), *The Boundless Sea: A Human History of the Oceans* (Oxford: Oxford University Press).

Alac, Patrik (2012), *Bikini Story* (New York: Parkstone Press International).

Allen, Woody (2016), *Crisis in Six Scenes*, Season 1, Episode 5, Amazon Prime Video, 30 September.

Aristotle (1980), trans. David Ross, *The Nicomachean Ethics* (Oxford: Oxford University Press).

Aristotle (no date), *The History of Animals*, trans. D'Arcy Wentworth Thompson <http://classics.mit.edu/Aristotle/history_anim.mb.txt>.

Aureli, Pier Vittorio (2011), *The Possibility of an Absolute Architecture* (Cambridge, MA: The MIT Press).

Aureli, Pier Vittorio, and Tattara, Martino (2010), 'STOP CITY', *Perspecta*, Vol. 43, 47-53.

Beatty, Paul (2016), *The Sellout* (London: Oneworld Publications).

Berger, John (2009), *Why Look at Animals?* (London: Penguin).

Bloom, Harold (1997), *The Anxiety of Influence: A Theory of Poetry* (Oxford: Oxford University Press).

Boyer, Anne (2015), 'The Girls' City', 20-22, in Wah and De'Ath (eds.) (2015).

Brand, Dionne (2001), *A Map to the Door of No Return: Notes to Belonging* (Toronto: Vintage Canada).

Brown, Simone (2015), *Dark Matters: On the Surveillance of Blackness* (Durham, NC: Duke University Press).

Chance the Rapper (2016), in Joyce, 'Chance The Rapper Reveals

"Ultralight Beam" Was For G.O.O.D. Fridays', *Complex* < https://www.complex.com/pigeons-and-planes/2016/11/chance-the-rapper-bbc-1-radio-interview>.

Collins, John J. (2017), *The Invention of Judaism: Torah and Jewish Identity from Deuteronomy to Paul* (Oakland, CA: University of California Press).

Eshun, Kodwo (2018), 'Mark Fisher Memorial Lecture', Goldsmiths, University of London <https://repeaterbooks.com/watch-kodwo-eshuns-inaugural-mark-fisher-memorial-lecture/>.

Fanon, Frantz (1970 [1967]), *Black Skin, White Masks*, trans. Charles Lam Markmann (London: Picador).

Federici, Silvia (1975), *Wages against Housework* (Bristol: Falling Wall Press).

Femi, Caleb (2020), *Poor* (London: Penguin).

Filipovic, Elena (2017), *David Hammons: Bliz-aard Ball Sale* (London: Afterall Books).

Fisher-Tiné, Harald, and Whyte, Christine (2017), 'Introduction', in Fisher-Tiné (ed.) (2017).

Fisher-Tiné, Harald (2017), *Anxieties, Fear and Panic in Colonial Settings: Empires on the Verge of a Nervous Breakdown* (New York: Springer).

Greene, Matt (2020), *Jew(ish): A primer, a memoir, a manual, a plea* (Seattle, WA: Little A).

Grosz, Elizabeth (2001), *Architecture from the Outside: Essays on Virtual and Real Space* (Cambridge, MA: The MIT Press).

Hong, Grace Kyungwon (2015), *Death beyond Disavowal: The Impossible Politics of Difference* (Minneapolis: University of Minnesota Press).

Hyatt, Vera Lawrence, and Nettleford, Rex M. (eds.) (1994), *Race, Discourse and the Origin of the Americas: A New World View* (Washington, DC: Smithsonian Books).

Jacobson, Howard (2013), 'Howard Jacobson on Comedy and the Finkler Question', *Schwartz Media* <https://www.youtube.com/watch?v=CYoqciWkzBk>.

Jazeel, Tariq (2011), 'Spatializing Difference Beyond Cosmopolitanism: Rethinking Planetary Futures', *Theory, Culture and Society*, Vol. 28, Issue 5, 75-97.

Jetñil-Kijiner, Kathy, and Niviâna, Aka (no date), 'It's Time to Rise' < https://www.kathyjetnilkijiner.com/>.

Kendi, Ibram X. (2016), *Stamped from the Beginning: The Definitive History of Racist Ideas in America* (New York: Nation Books).

Kim, W. Chan, and Mauborgne, Renée (2015), *Blue Ocean Strategy, Expanded Edition: How to Create Uncontested Market Space and Make the Competition Irrelevant* (Cambridge, MA: Harvard Business Review Press).

King, Tiffany Lethabo, and Wilderson III, Frank B. (2020), 'Staying Ready for Black Study', 52-73, in King, Navarro, and Smith (2020).

King, Tiffany Lethabo, Navarro, Jenell, and Smith, Andrea (eds.) (2020), *Otherwise Worlds: Against Settler Colonialism and Anti-Blackness* (Durham, NC: Duke University Press).

King, Tiffany Lethabo (2019), *The Black Shoals: Offshore Formations of Black and Native Studies* (Durham, NC: Duke University Press).

Kipling, Rudyard (1899), 'The White Man's Burden: The United States & the Philippine Islands' <http://www.kiplingsociety. co.uk/poems_burden.htm>.

Kundnani, Arun (2014), *The Muslims Are Coming! Islamophobia, Extremism, and the Domestic War on Terror* (London: Verso).

Levey, Michael (1973 [1968]), *A History of Western Art* (London: Book Club Associates).

Lowell, Robert (2001 [1959]), *Life Studies* (London: Faber and Faber).

Marriott, David (2016), 'Corpsing; or, The Matter of Black Life', *Cultural Critique*, Vol. 94, 32-64.

Matsoukas, Melina (2019), *Queen & Slim* (USA: 3 Black Dot).

McKittrick, Katherine (ed.) (2015), *Sylvia Wynter: On Being Human as Praxis* (Durham, NC: Duke University Press).

McKittrick, Katherine (2006), *Demonic Grounds: Black Women and the Cartographies of Struggle* (Minneapolis, MN: The University of Minnesota Press).

Miller-Young, Mireille (2014), *A Taste for Brown Sugar: Black Women in Pornography* (London: Duke University Press).

Moten, Fred (2020), '"Wildcat the Totality": Fred Moten and Stefano Harney Revisit *The Undercommons* in a Time of Pandemic and Rebellion', *Millennials Are Killing Capitalism*, podcast <https://millennialsarekillingcapitalism.libsyn.com/>

Moten, Fred, and Perry, Sondra (2018), 'Fred Moten in conversation with Sondra Perry', *Frieze* Podcast <http://podcasts.frieze.com/?name=2018-12-10_fny18_talks_audio_fred_moten_and_sondra_perry.mp3>

Moten, Fred (2018), *Stolen Life* (Durham, NC: Duke University Press).

Moten, Fred (2018), *'come on, get it!* with Thom Donovan, Malik Gaines, Ethan Philbrick, Wikipedia and the Online Etymology Dictionary', *The New Inquiry* < https://thenewinquiry.com/come_on_get_it/>.

Moten, Fred (2008), 'The Case of Blackness', *Criticism*, Vol. 50, No. 2, 177-218.

Nash, Jennifer C. (2014), *The Black Body in Ecstasy: Reading Race, Reading Pornography* (Durham, NC: Duke University Press).

Ngai, Sianne (2005), *Ugly Feelings* (Cambridge, Mass.: Harvard University Press).

Niedenthal, Jack (no date), 'A Short History of the People of Bikini Atoll' <https://www.bikiniatoll.com/>.

Orwell, George (1936), 'Shooting an Elephant' < http://www.orwell.ru/library/articles/elephant/english/e_eleph>.

Pat-Borja, Melvin Won (no date), 'No Deal', in Santos Perez (2017).

Perera, Jessica (2018), *The London Clearances: Race, Housing and Policing* (London: The Institute of Race Relations) < https://irr.org.uk/app/uploads/2019/02/The-London-Clearances-Race-Housing-and-Policing.pdf>.

Philip, M. NourbeSe (2017), *Blank: Essays and Interviews* (Toronto:

BookThug Press).

Pokornowski, Stephen (2016), 'Vulnerable Life: Zombies, Global Biopolitics, and the Reproduction of Structural Violence', *Humanities*, Vol. 5, No. 71.

Preciado, Paul B. (2019), *An Apartment on Uranus*, trans. Charlotte Mandell (London: Fitzcarraldo Editions).

Puar, Jasbir K. (2015), 'Bodies with New Organs: Becoming Trans, Becoming Disabled', *Social Text*, Vol. 33, No. 3, 45-73.

Ramesh, Randeep (2007), 'India's secret history: "A holocaust, one where millions disappeared…"' in *The Guardian* < https://www. theguardian.com/world/2007/aug/24/india.randeepramesh>.

Ratajkowski, Emily (2016), 'Baby Woman', *Lenny* <https://www. lennyletter.com/story/emily-ratajkowski-baby-woman>.

Roberts, Brian Russell, and Stephens, Michelle Ann (eds.) (2017), *Archipelagic American Studies* (Durham, NC: Duke University Press).

Robinson, Cedric (2000 [1983]), *Black Marxism: The Making of the Black Radical Tradition* (Chapel Hill, NC: The University of North Carolina Press).

Rose, Jacqueline (2021), 'Damage: The silent forms of violence against women', in *The Guardian* <https://www.theguardian. com/news/2021/mar/30/damage-the-silent-forms-of-violence-against-women>.

Santos Perez, Craig (2017), 'Guam and Archipelagic American Studies', 106-107, in Roberts and Stephens (2017).

Schalansky, Judith (2012), *Pocket Atlas of Remote Islands: Fifty Islands I have not visited and never will* (London: Penguin).

Schultz, Ben (2003), *Ben Schultz's Field Guide to Saltwater Fish* (Hoboken, NJ: Wiley).

Sean (2019), 'Celebrating Female Anglers', FishingBooker blog <https://fishingbooker.com/blog/celebrating-female-anglers-womens-day-2019/>.

Self, Will (2014), 'The novel is dead (this time it's for real)', *The Guardian* <https://www.theguardian.com/books/2014/may/02/

will-self-novel-dead-literary-fiction>.

Sexton, Jared (2020), 'The *Vel* of Slavery: Tracking the Figure of the Unsovereign', 94-117, in King, Navarro, and Smith (2020).

Sexton, Jared (2011), 'The Social Life of Social Death: On Afro-Pessimism and Black Optimism', *InTensions Journal*, Issue 5, 1-47.

Shriver, Lionel (2018), in Cooke, Rachel, 'Lionel Shriver: "Few writers are willing to put themselves on the line for free speech"', *The Guardian* <https://www.theguardian.com/books/2018/apr/14/lionel-shriver-property-metoo-cultural-appropriation>.

Snorton, C. Riley (2017), *Black on Both Sides: A Racial History of Trans Identity* (Minneapolis, MN: University of Minnesota Press).

Stavridis, Admiral James (2017), *Sea Power: The History and Geopolitics of the World's Oceans* (London: Penguin).

Tadiar, Neferti X. M. (2016), 'City Everywhere', *Theory, Culture & Society*, Vol. 33, Issue 7-8, 57-83.

Tanizaki, Jun'ichirō (2001), *In Praise of Shadows*, trans. Thomas J. Harper and Edward G. Seidensticker (London: Vintage).

Urban Dictionary (2010), 'fishing' <https://www.urbandictionary.com/define.php?term=fishing>.

Vasari, Giorgio (1965), *Lives of the Artists*, trans. George Bull (Harmondsworth: Penguin).

Wah, Fred, and De'Ath, Amy (eds.) (2015), *Toward. Some. Air: Remarks on Poetics* (Banff, Alberta: Banff Centre Press).

Waithe, Lena (2019), on Noah, Trevor, 'Making Urgent Art About the Black Experience with "Queen & Slim"', *The Daily Show* <https://www.youtube.com/watch?v=5r6ZbBdGDu4>.

Watson, Emma (2017), in Chastain, Jessica, 'Emma Watson', *Interview Magazine* <https://www.interviewmagazine.com/film/emma-watson-1>.

Weil, Simone (2005), *An Anthology*, ed. Siân Miles (London: Penguin Classics).

Witherington III, Ben (2018), *Torah Old and New: Exegesis, Intertextuality, and Hermeneutics* (Minneapolis, MN: Fortress

Press).

Wynter, Sylvia, and McKittrick, Katherine (2015), 'Unparalleled Catastrophe for Our Species? Or, to Give Humanness a Different Future: Conversations', 9-89, in McKittrick (ed.) (2015).

Wynter, Sylvia (1994), '1492: A New World View', 5-57, in Hyatt and Nettleford (eds.) (1994).

Yusoff, Kathryn (2019), 'White Utopia / Black Inferno: Life on a Geological Spike', *e-flux*, #97 <https://www.e-flux.com/journal/97/252226/white-utopia-black-inferno-life-on-a-geologic-spike/>.

Further Reading

Lots of works that are crucial to my understanding of the issues discussed in this book have not been directly cited here. Some of them are too academic to be quoted in a book like this, and some need much more room to be properly engaged with than can be offered in these short pages.

If you are interested in the topic and would like to read further, here is a list of texts that are very important to me and my study practice but were not included in the list of references.

Abdurraqib, Hanif (2021), *A Little Devil in America: In Praise of Black Performance* (London: Allen Lane).

Agamben, Giorgio (2016), *The Use of Bodies*, trans. Adam Kotsko (Stanford, CA: Stanford University Press).

Arrighi, Giovanni (1994), *The Long Twentieth Century: Money, Power, and the Origins of Our Times* (London: Verso).

Baucom, Ian (2005), *Specters of the Atlantic: Finance Capital, Slavery, and the Philosophy of History* (Durham, NC: Duke University Press).

Baucom, Ian (1999), *Out of Place: Englishness, Empire, and the Locations of Identity* (Princeton, NJ: Princeton University Press).

Bhandar, Brenna (2018), *Colonial Lives of Property: Law, Land, and Racial Regimes of Ownership* (Durham, NC: Duke University Press).

Bliss, Eula (2021), *Having and Being Had* (London: Faber and Faber).

Bratton, Benjamin H. (2015), *Dispute Plan to Prevent Future Luxury Construction* (Berlin: Sternberg Press).

Brown, Adrienne (2017), *The Black Skyscraper: Architecture and the Perception of Race* (Baltimore, MD: Johns Hopkins University Press).

Brown, Adrienne, and Smith, Valerie (eds.) (2016), *Race and Real Estate* (Oxford: Oxford University Press).

Carter, J. Kameron (2008), *Race: A Theological Account* (Oxford: Oxford University Press).

Cavarero, Adriana (2016), *Inclinations: A Critique of Rectitude* (Stanford, CA: Stanford University Press).

Chandler, Nahum D. (2018), 'Paraontology; or, Notes on the Practical Theoretical Politics of Thought' <https://vimeo.com/297769615>.

Cheng, Anne Anlin (2019), *Ornamentalism* (Oxford: Oxford University Press).

Cheng, Irene, Davis II, Charles L., and Wilson, Mabel O. (eds.) (2020), *Race and Modern Architecture: A Critical History from the Enlightenment to the Present* (Pittsburgh, PA: University of Pittsburgh Press).

Cohen, Tom, Colebrook, Claire, and Miller, J. Hillis (2016), *Twilight of the Anthropocene Idols* (London: Open Humanities Press).

Coulthard, Glen Sean (2014), *Red Skin, White Masks: Rejecting the Colonial Politics of Recognition* (Minneapolis, MN: University of Minnesota Press).

Davis, Angela Y. (2019 [1981]), *Women, Race & Class* (London: Penguin).

Davis II, Charles L. (2019), *Building Character: The Racial Politics of Modern Architectural Style* (Pittsburgh, PA.: University of Pittsburgh Press).

Ferreira da Silva, Denise (2018), 'In the Raw', *e-flux*, no. 93 <https://www.e-flux.com/journal/93/215795/in-the-raw/>.

Ferreira da Silva, Denise (2014), 'Toward a Black Feminist Poethics: The Quest(ion) of Blackness Toward the End of the World', *The Black Scholar*, 44:2, 81-97.

Ferreira da Silva, Denise (2014), 'No Bodies: Law, Raciality and Violence', *Meritum*, Belo Horizonte, Vol. 9, No. 1, 119-162.

Ferreira da Silva, Denise (2007), *Toward a Global Idea of Race*

(Minneapolis, MN: University of Minnesota Press).

Fields, Darell Wayne (2015 [2000]), *Architecture in Black: Theory, Space, and Appearance* (London: Bloomsbury).

Gilroy, Paul (1993), *The Black Atlantic: Modernity and Double Consciousness* (London: Verso).

Glissant, Édouard (1997 [1990]), *Poetics of Relation*, trans. Betsy Wing (Ann Arbor, MI: The University of Michigan Press).

Goldsby, Jacqueline (2006), *A Spectacular Secret: Lynching in American Life and Literature* (Chicago: University of Chicago Press).

Gómez-Barris, Macarena (2017), *The Extractive Zone: Social Ecologies and Decolonial Perspectives* (Durham, NC: Duke University Press).

Grant, Melissa Gira (2014), *Playing the Whore: The Work of Sex Work* (London: Verso).

Halpern, Rob (2012), *Music for Porn* (New York: Nightboat Books).

Hartman, Saidiya V. (2019), *Wayward Lives, Beautiful Experiments* (New York: W. W. Norton & Company).

Hartman, Saidiya V. (1997), *Scenes of Subjection: Terror, Slavery, and Self-Making in Nineteenth-Century America* (Oxford: Oxford University Press).

hooks, bell (1992), *Black Looks: Race and Representation* (Boston, MA: South End Press).

Jackson, Zakiyyah Iman (2020), *Becoming Human: Matter and Meaning in an Antiblack World* (New York: New York University Press).

Ladkin, Sam (2015), 'The "Onanism of Poetry"', *Angelaki*, Vol. 20, Issue 4, 131-156.

Lloyd, David (2019), *Under Representation: The Racial Regime of Aesthetics* (New York: Fordham University Press).

Mbembe, Achille (2017), *Critique of Black Reason*, trans. Laurent Dubois (Durham, NC: Duke University Press).

Mirzoeff, Nicholas (2011), *The Right to Look: A Counterhistory to*

Visuality (London and Durham, NC: Duke University Press).

Morrison, Toni (1992), *Playing in the Dark* (Cambridge, MA: Harvard University Press).

Moten, Fred (2018), *The Universal Machine*, (Durham, NC: Duke University Press).

Moten, Fred (2017), *Black and Blur*, (Durham, NC: Duke University Press).

Moten, Fred, and Tsang, Wu (2015), 'Who Touched Me?', *If I Can't Dance I Don't Want to be Part of Your Revolution*, Performance in Residence < https://ificantdance.org/product/who-touched-me/>.

Moten, Fred (2015), *The Little Edges* (Middletown, CT: Wesleyan University Press).

Philip, M. NourbeSe (2011), *Zong!* (Middletown, CT: Wesleyan University Press).

Pitts, Johny (2020), *Afropean: Notes from Black Europe* (London: Penguin).

Power, Nina (2009), *One Dimensional Woman* (Ropley, Hants.: Zer0 Books).

Povinelli, Elizabeth A. (2016), *Geontologies: A Requiem to Late Liberalism* (Durham, NC: Duke University Press).

Preciado, Paul B. (2019), *Pornotopia: An Essay on Playboy's Architecture and Biopolitics* (New York: Zone Books).

Rankine, Claudia (2020), *Just Us: An American Conversation* (London: Allen Lane).

Rondilla, Joanne L., Guevarra Jr., Rudy P., and Spickard, Paul (2017), *Red and Yellow, Black and Brown: Decentering Whiteness in Mixed Race Studies* (New Brunswick, NJ: Rutgers University Press).

Sharpe, Christina, *In the Wake: On Blackness and Being* (Durham, NC: Duke University Press, 2016).

Spillers, Hortense J. (1987), 'Mama's Baby, Papa's Maybe: An American Grammar Book', *Diacritics*, Vol. 19, No. 2, 64-81.

Taylor, Keeanga-Yamahtta (2019), *Race for Profit: How Banks and the Real Estate Industry Undermined Black Homeownership* (Chapel Hill, NC: The University of North Carolina Press).

Weheliye, Alexander G. (2014), *Habeas Viscus: Racializing Assemblages, Biopolitics, and Black Feminist Theories of the Human* (Durham, NC: Duke University Press).

Wilderson III, Frank B. (2020), *Afro-pessimism* (New York: Liveright Publishing).

Yusoff, Kathryn (2018), *A Billion Black Anthropocenes or None* (Minneapolis, MN: University of Minnesota Press).

Glossary

This is not an academic book, but some terms are used from academic language. For clarity, below are brief descriptions of how I use these words in this book.

* * *

Capital/capitalism: at school (in the UK at least), we do not learn what capitalism is, and we are not told that we live in capitalism. Naturally, this produces confusion later in life. Capitalism is not the same as trade or exchange or selfishness or profit. Capitalism is a very specific way of organizing society, using a precise economic mode. That mode is *exchange value*. In other ways of organizing societies, commodities have *use value*—their value depends on how they can be used; so, for example, a guitar can be traded with a dining chair dependent on how useful each object is. If you are a guitarist, one guitar is worth many chairs. But if you cannot play the guitar and you enjoy hosting big dinners, then chairs are much more valuable than guitars. In capitalism, however, every single commodity only has *exchange value*—it is valuable only in relation to one universal commodity (which is the given equivalent of all things on earth): money. In later stages of capitalism, this logic applies not only to physical commodities but to everything, including beliefs, dreams, stories, feelings, and time itself. Money can then make money out of money by investing in the promise of more profit in the future, which is the fundamental strategy of investment capitalism. When money is invested in the future, it is called capital; capital is the accumulated belief in more production in the future than now.

 Epistemology: the study of knowledge. Something that is *epistemological* is something that concerns the structure and meaning of knowledge. Fundamental epistemological questions would be something like: How can things be known? What is knowledge? How is it that we know things, rather than believe or experience things?

Feminization: Instead of referring to things that are usually called *female* as *female*, in this book I refer to them as *feminized*. What this word attempts to portray is the absence of any *nature* to the binaries of gender. If a person, for example, is simply *female*, we presume that her state within gender is natural and unchanging. She is, always, *female*, like the moon in French, or the sea in Spanish poetry: *la mar*. However, my proposition, alongside many others who propose the same thing, is that gender is not a natural state that is already given to a person. Gender is something that is learnt and structurally imposed through language, politics, culture, and the economy over many generations. Certain cultural acts and aesthetic symbols become *feminized* through a culture and economy that require division and simple systems of labelling. The structure of the feminizing and misogynist capitalist state that can be summed up as 'the patriarchy' relies on a large part of the population being trained as machines for reproducing workers, and for circulating and exchanging value in certain *feminized* ways—and that part of the population is called *women*, or what I refer to in this book, after Amy De'Ath, as *feminized people*.

Liberal/liberalism: the term *liberal* is often taken to simply mean *left-wing*, in a world in which there are only two political opinions: *liberal/left* or *conservative/right*. In certain social circles, *liberal* is synonymous with *good*. In this book, I mean *liberal* as the adjective of the noun *liberalism*, and *liberalism* is a specific political tradition, which is historically bound to capitalism. It began in the eighteenth century, with the emergence of the modern notion of humanity as a set of self-interested individuals who exist to trade and to accumulate property, which was a very new idea at the time.

In this kind of *liberalism*, both conservatives and liberals are *liberal*, since they both broadly believe in the capitalist idea of politics functioning through the economy, and the economy functioning through exchange value (see the description of *capitalism* above). The position that is not *liberal* is *radical* (see the description below).

Modernity: Modernity in this book refers to the era of imperial, cartographic capitalism, since the middle of the fifteenth century, and then emphasized through the narrative of normative science since the second half of the eighteenth century. When Europeans began colonizing other lands and establishing a single idea of the World in the fifteenth century, the current human way of thinking was simultaneously established. Life became an expansive pursuit of growing territory, on national and personal scales. The kind of expansive and dominating subjectivity that accompanies this geographical movement was affirmed by the European Enlightenment and the post-Enlightenment philosophy of reason. Essentially, what these changes created is the ability for each human to imagine the possibility of universal reach. Claims are often made in Euro-American culture today, for example, that 'God is dead', claiming a single trajectory of belief throughout the planet and the species, as if all life followed the particular belief system of Euro-American White bourgeois life. For other cultures — cultures ignored by these universalizing claims of modernity — there was never such a self-convinced moment of God's dramatic death.

Ontology: the study of being. Something *ontological* is something that concerns the structure and nature of being. Ontological questions that reverberate throughout philosophy are things like: How is it that we are alive? How is it that things *are* rather than *are not*? Why is there existence? I am not concerned with these kinds of questions in this book, but there is a lot of *ontological* questioning, which investigates the structure of being of certain things in the world, like asking how they came into existence and why they continue to exist.

Racialization: in a similar way to how the word *feminization* attempts to dislodge the apparent nature of gender, *racialization* is a way of emphasizing the imposed construction of race. Race is not natural. In fact, as I write in this book, it is the other way around: *nature is racial. Racialization* refers to the long history of how the social referent that is *race* came to have such profound meaning for the way humans understand society and ourselves today. Since the fifteenth century, when Europeans began the colonial project and changed the meaning of the planet into a single World, certain physical and ontological signifiers of the human body and the human experience of having a body have referred to absolute notions of race, which have categorized a person's and a people's proximity to violence; turning them into slaves or into masters, into property or into property-owners, and eternalizing this state for their kin.

Many texts have been written about the history of race and racialization. Find references to them in this book itself, or in the Further Reading section.

Radical/radicalism: in general conversation, if you say 'radical' then you are probably a Californian surfer, or at least wearing humid shorts. The British version of the same person calls everything 'savage' — e.g.: *this pickled eel and mash is savage, mate.* In this book, however, and in philosophy generally, *radicalism* is the position that is against politics. Within liberal politics, you can be either right-wing or left-wing; conservative or, confusingly, liberal, to varying extremes. But there is another position of belief, which is that all of politics is a function of the capitalist economy and the kind of subjectivity it creates, limiting people's engagement with each other to the mediation of the market and the profit-productive subjectivity that can only think of value as exchange value. Radicals want a different system; a system in which value is given through an alternative mode of subjectivity. Precisely what that system and that subjectivity is, though, not many radicals agree on.

Violence: in philosophy, *violence* means something slightly different to what it means in general usage. In this context, violence refers to a rupture in the path of coherent beliefs. It is much more general, and more complex, than the everyday violence of punching a wall. Any structuring social belief—capitalism, Christmas, religion, football, socialism—requires a trajectory of collective investment, which brings people's beliefs together as one overarching concept. A violent act is one that ruptures that belief. The possibility of such a belief as socialism is violence against capitalism, because capitalism cannot coexist with a general belief in revolutionary socialism. Likewise, overcharging someone for a product or making someone work a little extra for free is an act of violence because structuring social relations are ruptured by the logics of profit and exploitation.

CULTURE, SOCIETY & POLITICS

The modern world is at an impasse. Disasters scroll across our smartphone screens and we're invited to like, follow or upvote, but critical thinking is harder and harder to find. Rather than connecting us in common struggle and debate, the internet has sped up and deepened a long-standing process of alienation and atomization. Zer0 Books wants to work against this trend. With critical theory as our jumping off point, we aim to publish books that make our readers uncomfortable. We want to move beyond received opinions.

Zer0 Books is on the left and wants to reinvent the left. We are sick of the injustice, the suffering and the stupidity that defines both our political and cultural world, and we aim to find a new foundation for a new struggle.

If this book has helped you to clarify an idea, solve a problem or extend your knowledge, you may want to check out our online content as well. Look for Zer0 Books: Advancing Conversations in the iTunes directory and for our Zer0 Books YouTube channel.

Popular videos include:

Žižek and the Double Blackmain

The Intellectual Dark Web is a Bad Sign

Can there be an Anti-SJW Left?

Answering Jordan Peterson on Marxism

Follow us on Facebook
at https://www.facebook.com/ZeroBooks and Twitter at https://
twitter.com/Zer0Books

Bestsellers from Zer0 Books include:

Give Them An Argument
Logic for the Left
Ben Burgis
Many serious leftists have learned to distrust talk of logic. This is
a serious mistake.
Paperback: 978-1-78904-210-8 ebook: 978-1-78904-211-5

Poor but Sexy
Culture Clashes in Europe East and West
Agata Pyzik
How the East stayed East and the West stayed West.
Paperback: 978-1-78099-394-2 ebook: 978-1-78099-395-9

An Anthropology of Nothing in Particular
Martin Demant Frederiksen
A journey into the social lives of meaninglessness.
Paperback: 978-1-78535-699-5 ebook: 978-1-78535-700-8

In the Dust of This Planet
Horror of Philosophy vol. 1
Eugene Thacker
In the first of a series of three books on the Horror of Philosophy,
In the Dust of This Planet offers the genre of horror as a way of
thinking about the unthinkable.
Paperback: 978-1-84694-676-9 ebook: 978-1-78099-010-1

The End of Oulipo?
An Attempt to Exhaust a Movement
Lauren Elkin, Veronica Esposito
Paperback: 978-1-78099-655-4 ebook: 978-1-78099-656-1

Capitalist Realism
Is There No Alternative?
Mark Fisher
An analysis of the ways in which capitalism has presented itself
as the only realistic political-economic system.
Paperback: 978-1-84694-317-1 ebook: 978-1-78099-734-6

Rebel Rebel
Chris O'Leary
David Bowie: every single song. Everything you want to know,
everything you didn't know.
Paperback: 978-1-78099-244-0 ebook: 978-1-78099-713-1

Kill All Normies
Angela Nagle
Online culture wars from 4chan and Tumblr to Trump.
Paperback: 978-1-78535-543-1 ebook: 978-1-78535-544-8

Romeo and Juliet in Palestine
Teaching Under Occupation
Tom Sperlinger
Life in the West Bank, the nature of pedagogy and the role of a
university under occupation.
Paperback: 978-1-78279-637-4 ebook: 978-1-78279-636-7

Ghosts of My Life
Writings on Depression, Hauntology and Lost Futures
Mark Fisher
Paperback: 978-1-78099-226-6 ebook: 978-1-78279-624-4

Sweetening the Pill
or How We Got Hooked on Hormonal Birth Control
Holly Grigg-Spall
Has contraception liberated or oppressed women?
Sweetening the Pill breaks the silence on the dark side of hormonal
contraception.
Paperback: 978-1-78099-607-3 ebook: 978-1-78099-608-0

Why Are We The Good Guys?
Reclaiming Your Mind from the Delusions of Propaganda
David Cromwell
A provocative challenge to the standard ideology that Western
power is a benevolent force in the world.
Paperback: 978-1-78099-365-2 ebook: 978-1-78099-366-9

The Writing on the Wall
On the Decomposition of Capitalism and its Critics
Anselm Jappe, Alastair Hemmens
A new approach to the meaning of social emancipation.
Paperback: 978-1-78535-581-3 ebook: 978-1-78535-582-0

Enjoying It
Candy Crush and Capitalism
Alfie Bown
A study of enjoyment and of the enjoyment of studying. Bown asks what enjoyment says about us and what we say about enjoyment, and why.
Paperback: 978-1-78535-155-6 ebook: 978-1-78535-156-3

Color, Facture, Art and Design
Iona Singh
This materialist definition of fine-art develops guidelines for architecture, design, cultural-studies and ultimately social change.
Paperback: 978-1-78099-629-5 ebook: 978-1-78099-630-1

Neglected or Misunderstood
The Radical Feminism of Shulamith Firestone
Victoria Margree
An interrogation of issues surrounding gender, biology, sexuality, work and technology, and the ways in which our imaginations continue to be in thrall to ideologies of maternity and the nuclear family.
Paperback: 978-1-78535-539-4 ebook: 978-1-78535-540-0

How to Dismantle the NHS in 10 Easy Steps (Second Edition)
Youssef El-Gingihy
The story of how your NHS was sold off and why you will have to buy private health insurance soon. A new expanded second edition with chapters on junior doctors' strikes and government blueprints for US-style healthcare.
Paperback: 978-1-78904-178-1 ebook: 978-1-78904-179-8

Digesting Recipes
The Art of Culinary Notation
Susannah Worth
A recipe is an instruction, the imperative tone of the expert, but
this constraint can offer its own kind of potential. A recipe need
not be a domestic trap but might instead offer escape – something
to fantasise about or aspire to.

Paperback: 978-1-78279-860-6 ebook: 978-1-78279-859-0

Most titles are published in paperback and as an ebook.
Paperbacks are available in traditional bookshops. Both print and
ebook formats are available online.
Follow us on Facebook
at https://www.facebook.com/ZeroBooks
and Twitter at https://twitter.com/Zer0Books